INTENDED CONSEQUENCES

INTENDED
CONSEQUENCES

A Novel
(Or is it?)

CHARLES D. GEORGE

Liberty Hill Publishing

Liberty Hill Publishing
2301 Lucien Way #415
Maitland, FL 32751
407.339.4217
www.libertyhillpublishing.com

Unless otherwise indicated, Scripture quotations taken from the King James Version (KJV)—*public domain.*

Paperback ISBN-13: 978-1-6628-3000-6
Ebook ISBN-13: 978-1-662-83001-3

Table of Contents

→→ Preface ←←

Everything which happens in the world has a cause-and-effect relationship. When you hear or read something has happened, and you think about the effect of the event, do you ever consider what might be the real cause of the event? Do you just accept the explanation given to you by the government or the media? Whether you like to believe conservative or progressive sources, do you question the veracity of what you are being told?

In day and age of 24/7 television news, every news source is trying to be the first to reach you with the story and give their explanation for the events. Often, what you are told about the cause of the event turns out not to be true or only part of the story. Occasionally the real reason for something happening is never known or revealed. What the public sees on television and reads in newspapers sometimes turns out to be intentionally misleading or fake news.

In this novel, Special Agent Douglas Gregory of the Federal Bureau of Investigation finds himself in situations where he has access to intelligence and major business contacts, providing him with insights to the cause of world events not reported in the news. The information he has access to may help explain a different cause or reason for some of the recent world and domestic events.

Sometimes the cause of an event is intentional, and the consequence planned to result in the control of a group of people or a political situation. When it is a domestic or foreign government, a major corporation, or an individual with a lot of money and power, the public can lose some or eventually all their freedoms and fundamental rights. This story will give you reason to question everything you hear from the government and the media, and to look for the truth. Remember, "The truth shall make you free" (John 8:32).

➤➤ Prologue ◄◄

It was March, but spring had not yet come to the nation's capital. The cherry trees were still a couple of weeks away from blooming. Washington, DC, was in the throes of the change of seasons. Today was one of those nasty, rain days, just cold enough to make it uncomfortable to be out and about.

Senator Robert Wagner (D) of New York was making his way down Wisconsin Avenue for an early morning meeting. He was driving himself in his 1940 Cadillac Fleetwood. Because of his leadership position and seniority in the Democrat-controlled US Senate, he would have normally had a driver pick him up for a trip to the White House (WH). However, since this meeting was off the record and very few people on the president's staff even knew about the meeting, the senator was traveling alone. As he turned into the driveway of the Executive Office Building, the Secret Service recognized him and waived him through to the parking lot behind the building. Entering the WH through the West Wing, he was immediately taken to the elevator and up to the president's living quarters.

Wagner was somewhat surprised to find Lieutenant Colonel William Bacon, from the Army's Chemical

Warfare Center at the Edgewood Arsenal, already in the second-floor meeting room. The Senator greeted Colonel Bacon, and then they sat quietly, waiting for their host. Neither knew exactly what the other one knew about the subject of this meeting. A few minutes later, President Roosevelt was wheeled into the meeting room.

"Good morning, Mr. President" was voiced by both visitors, almost simultaneously. Both were directed to sit down.

Franklin Delano Roosevelt, the thirty-second president of the United States, and the people of the country were in the middle of a World War (WW) they really did not want to be in. The US avoided participation in the war, which began in Europe almost four years earlier, until the Japanese bombed Pearl Harbor on December 7, 1941. Now the US was involved. Concerns about chemical warfare used in WWI were resurfacing. There was a lot of opposition in the country about the possible use of chemicals in this war. Adolf Hitler and the Nazis knew this, but the fact did not constrain them. Intelligence reached the Allies that the Germans had undertaken a biological weapons research program. The German war machine saw US public opinion as a weakness and decided they might be able to use this to their advantage in the war against enemies in Europe as well as in the United States.

FDR and Senator Wagner were long-time acquaintances and friends. The president had been in office since 1933. Wagner had been a member of the Senate since 1927. They were both from New York State, and both were Tammany Hall politicians. The president knew he could rely on the senator. He also knew he could rely on Lieutenant Colonel Bacon, who had been thoroughly vetted.

"Gentlemen, we are about to engage in something, which may permanently affect not only the citizens of our country, but those of the whole world."

The president then laid out the plans for the development of the US Army Biological Warfare Laboratories (USBWL). The lab would be responsible for pioneering research into not only biocontainment, decontamination, gaseous sterilization, and agent purification, but also the surreptitious development of pathogens. Both men listening to the president already knew the latter was something that was "out of bounds" and would have to be kept from the public.

In November 1942, the president had already directed Secretary of War Henry Stimson to form the War Research Service (WRS) as a cover for coordinating and supervising a US biological warfare program. Just like the super-secret Manhattan Project that was approved by FDR back in 1939, this research would be developed under the strictest security measures. A former Army Airfield just fifty miles northeast of Washington, DC, had been chosen as the location for this program. Fort Detrick, in Frederick, Maryland, would become the first site for USBWL program.

The president had chosen Senator Wagner to be the only person in the US Senate to be privy to this project. Not only because of the senator's long-standing relationship with FDR, but he was known to be trustworthy. Also, because Wagner had a personal relationship with George W. Merck who was the son of the founder of the Merck & Co. Inc., a multi-national pharmaceutical company. Merck was the company's current president and had agreed to oversee the laboratory work at the USBWL. Lieutenant Colonel Bacon would be the military commander of the facility, responsible for the security of the post and projects.

When the president finished his briefing he said, "Gentlemen, thank you for coming in."

The president did not give either of his visitors the opportunity to ask any questions. They stood up and followed the president's aide to the elevator. Moments later, they were outside walking to the parking lot, still not sure what to say to each other. The traffic on the streets of the District (Washington, DC) had picked up, but the rain had let up. Senator Wagner headed for the Capitol. Colonel Bacon drove to Frederick, Maryland, to survey what he was about to assume command of.

The original facility, known as Detrick Field until 1942, was just ninety-two acres and served as one of a string of emergency airfields and as a training base for the US Army Air Corps. In 1941, the government purchased an additional 154 acres of land for the USBWL, and the post was redesignated as Fort Detrick. Initially, a modest $ 1.25 million was provided for the renovation of the post. Three months after the construction began, another $3 million, partly appropriated funds and the rest in "black money," was provided for five laboratories and a pilot plant. The research was classified, and the work took all kinds of forms. Some of which would have been considered as non-controversial and some prohibited.

At the peak in 1945, Colonel Bacon had 1,770 military personnel under his command, not including the scientists and civilian employees who were working for the pharmaceutical companies doing research in the laboratories. Merck recruited Ira Baldwin, a professor of bacteriology at the University of Wisconsin, as the first scientific director of the labs. Baldwin's job was to give an appearance of promoting public security and health. In reality, the WRS was responsible for coordinating and supervising the US biological warfare effort.

The 1925 Geneva Protocol banning bacteriological warfare had been ratified by most of the major power countries but had not been ratified by the US Senate. This was because of strong lobbying by the WRS and pharmaceutical companies like Merck. Thanks to the work of Senator Wagner, the ratification of the treaty was never brought to the Senate floor for a vote.

Research was kept under wraps so well that it was not until January 1946, which was four months after Victory over Japan (V-J Day), that the public learned of the wartime research into biological weapons for the first time. The public learned about the Manhattan

Project in August 1945, when President Harry Truman ordered the first atomic bombs dropped on Hiroshima and Nagasaki. The fact that the US did not use any pathogens during WWII may have been the reason Americans didn't seem concerned with the secret biological laboratory work during the war. Americans were more concerned with what the development of the atomic bomb might portend. The research work continued at Fort Detrick unabated.

In the period following WWII, Fort Detrick was still a hub of activity. During the war Dietrick had become the site of what was described as intensive biological warfare. It was cloaked in the deepest secrecy, matching the security of the Manhattan Project. The Army's Chemical Warfare Service took over responsibility for oversight of the USBWL.

From 1945 to 1955, under an operation called "Project Paperclip," the US government recruited German and Austrian scientists from a number of fields, including biological warfare. Many of these scientists had been involved in experiments on American and allied concentration camp prisoners of war to test biological warfare agents.

During the post-war period two workers at Ft. Detrick died from exposure to anthrax and another from viral encephalitis. Building 470 on the post, referred to as the "Anthrax Tower," was the pilot plant for testing optimal fermenter and bacterial purification technologies. It would eventually be removed for safety reasons. To the workers on the post and to those in the know, Detrick became known as "Fort Doom."

Scientists from Detrick conducted hundreds of thousands of tests on human subjects, involving hazardous substances, in what was known as "Operation Whitecoat." Originally the subjects were volunteer enlisted soldiers. As more information surfaced about the dangers of the biological tests a church group of conscientious objectors were recruited for the test studies. Other covert field testing of biological weapons in September 1950 included large-scale spraying of stimulants and agents over wide areas, including the San Francisco Bay area. Experiments were also conducted in the subways of New York City in 1966. This continued until 1974.

As information about the biological weapons programs began to leak out, the members of the science community were beginning to turn against such research. However, the general populous continued to remain largely uninformed about the results of the work until it became public again during the Vietnam War. During that war, the use of riot-control agents and herbicides, such as Agent Orange, drew international criticism. This negatively affected public opinion regarding the use of biological weapons. As a result, President Nixon's administration felt a need to respond to the growing negative perception of the development of biological weapons. In November 1969, the president decreed the US would end the biological research program, and all biological weapons would be destroyed, except for research of defense-only agents. Nixon entered into the international Biological Weapons Convention that outlawed biological warfare. In 1975 the United States also ratified the 1925 Geneva Protocol.

When the US biological warfare program ended in 1969, it had developed six mass-produced biological weapons, all of which were battle ready. Twenty more agents were capable of being weaponized. Included among these twenty agents were several strains of coronavirus. Since these viruses had not been weaponized, they were not on the list of biological weapons disposed of by the researchers at Fort Detrick. Classified research continued on the coronaviruses under the command of the US Army Medical Research Institute of Infectious Diseases (USAMRIID). It was eventually shut down by the Centers for Disease Control and Prevention (CDC), but the writing was already on the wall. The relationship of the American pharmaceutical companies working with the USAMRIID at Fort Detrick and those involved with the research at the Wuhan Institute of Virology in China was incestuous. Much of the US viral technology had already been transferred to the Wuhan lab, along with 3.6 million dollars from the National Institute of Health to fund continuing research.

➤➤ Chapter 1 ◄◄

Fall is always an exciting time on the campus of The Ohio State University (OSU). The trees and the buildings around the Oval on campus make it one of the most beautiful in the country. Freshmen arrive on campus for orientation and upper-class students return for another year of academics and football. Make no mistake, the latter activity is part of the magic that draws a lot of students from the Buckeye State to Columbus, Ohio, for their collegiate experience. This year the men of the Scarlet and Grey football team were expected to compete for the Big Ten title and possibly a national championship. Everyone was looking forward to what was ahead for them, including Daniel Chen. He was a foreign student from Mainland China.

Chen was a couple of years older than most of the freshman students entering college. He appeared younger than his age and seemed to fit in well with the other students. His English was exceptionally good, and he communicated well with everyone he encountered. Chen was obviously also very bright and came to OSU to study biology. Even though he was very proficient in English, like all freshman students without college credits in English, he was required to enroll in English 1101.01. It was there he met fellow freshman, Douglas Gregory, from Hamilton, Ohio.

All first-year students at Ohio State, except those who are married or from the Columbus area and live at home, are required to live in a dorm. Gregory was assigned to Archer Hall. Chen and Gregory were not in the same dorm, nor were they in the same academic program, but on the first day of English class, they happened to sit next to each other. Right out of the box, the graduate student teaching the class assigned a paperback book to read. She told the students they would briefly discuss the book the following week and then would be writing a book review. Chen asked Gregory if he had the book. He did. Chen then wanted to know where he could obtain a copy. Gregory told him after class he would take him to the bookstore so he could buy one.

After class, they walked across the Oval to the bookstore at 15th and High Streets. Gregory was an inquisitive type and learned from Chen he was from near Beijing. Being from a bedroom community in southwest Ohio, Gregory had little contact with Asians and no previous contact with anyone he knew was a Chinese native. He was fascinated Chen's English was so good and tried to get into Chen's background a little more. Chen seemed reluctant to discuss much about his life. The bookstore still had plenty of used copies of the paperback book he needed for class. Gregory had another class in less than an hour in Hagerty Hall, so he headed to the Ohio Union on High Street, while Chen went back to his dorm.

In high school, Gregory had taken Spanish for college credit, and because of that, he was exempt from the foreign language requirement of the business school curriculum. Gregory was not interested in taking more Spanish in college and was not sure about the need to take another foreign language. However, he heard Mandarin Chinese was easy to learn, so he thought he would ask Chen to teach him a little of the language. Gregory would decide later whether to take a Chinese class or some other foreign language.

After their next English class, Gregory mention, to Chen about possibly taking a Chinese language class. Chen seemed proud to share his native language. There was no time for formal tutoring or anything on a regular schedule. So as not to interfere with their other studies, Chen agreed to meet Gregory in the Ohio Union a couple of times a week for an hour. Learning some conversational phrases would come first. While the phrases were easy enough to remember, Gregory learned very quickly the pronunciation of phases was the important factor in speaking the language. Unlike English, Mandarin is a tonal language and mastering the four main tones of the language is key to expressing yourself in the Mandarin. *Zaoshang hao* and *zao an* (good morning), and *zaijian* and *baibai* (goodbye and bye, respectively) became common phases Gregory would practice every day. He would use them with his friends in the dorm, even though no one knew what he was saying. Over the period of the semester, Doug Gregory picked up a lot of phrases he would use.

When the second term began, Chen and Gregory were in different English classes, although they would occasionally run into each other on campus, and thus, the Mandarin language meetings did not continue. They were on different academic paths and had different social lives. When you live on campus, the dormitory is the center of your social universe unless you join a fraternity of sorority. Gregory was not a fraternity man, and he did not have a clue about Chen's social life.

As luck would have it, during their sophomore year, Chen was in a Political Science class with Gregory. This was an elective for Gregory since the class was not part of the Fisher Business College curriculum. Gregory was planning to go to law school and thought every lawyer should be schooled in the world of politics, but he thought it a little strange Chen was taking Poly Sci since Chen was a science major. Chen said he found American politics very interesting and was looking forward to presenting in class a comparative analysis of his country's government with that of the US system. Gregory did not press the subject. It was good to see an acquaintance. They agreed to get together for a chat. Chen had moved off campus his second year, but Gregory was still in a dormitory. They agreed again to meet at the Ohio Union.

When they met Gregory immediately greeted Chen with "zao an" even though it was mid-afternoon. There is no Chinese expression for a midday greeting. They talked about their first year at Ohio State and the past summer. Chen went to summer school, and Gregory had gone home to Hamilton to work for the summer. Chen seemed to be well financed at school while Gregory had limited resources and needed to work for school money. Chen wanted to know if Gregory had enrolled in a Chinese class. He was disappointed to learn Gregory had not, so he began encouraging his friend to consider taking a class and gave him the name of a graduate instructor to take a class from. Since Chen was a Chinese native, he would probably not be taking Chinese language classes, but obviously he had made some Chinese contacts during his first year at Ohio State. Gregory said he was still considering it and indicated his schedule next year might be better for the endeavor.

This time Chen seemed to take more of an interest in what Gregory was planning after college. Gregory indicated he was not entirely sure what he wanted to do after law school, but he talked about possibly going into politics. There was no father's law firm back home he could step into. He would be starting at the bottom of whatever he did.

Chen also seemed to be a little more open about his situation. He said his father was a low-ranking public figure in the Hebei Province, which nearly surrounds the capital city of his country. This allowed him to go to a special school for children of politicians, where he excelled as a science student. He was given a full government scholarship to study at a US university. The decision what to study was his, but which university he attended was decided for him by a government committee. He was only vaguely familiar with The Ohio State University before he came to Columbus but now enjoyed being here. After graduation, he planned to attend graduate school and work on advanced degrees in microbiology. Where he would go to graduate school after Ohio State also depended on a government committee.

Chen also talked a little about his extracurricular interest. He indicated he was not a rabid football fan, like most of the OSU students appeared to be, but he did like to go to the Buckeye basketball games. Basketball is big in China, and his country fields good basketball teams in the Olympics and in international competition. He mentioned his social life was somewhat muted because of concentration on his studies and because it has been difficult to find American girls who want to date Chinese men. Most of his social contact was with the Chinese female students he met at what is called "The China House" near campus. It is not an officially approved university organization but functions more as just a place where Chinese students gather if they miss being at home or just want to contact other students and teachers from China.

Gregory was doing well academically, but his social life was kind of a drag. He did not have a car, so dating was getting one of the dorm girls to go to a movie or finding something to do at the Ohio Union. He was still not of drinking age, so hanging out on Friday nights at the beer drinking and pizza places on High Street was not in the cards. In the fall, Saturday meant football in the Shoe. Sundays were usually devoted to just relaxing and listening to classical music. In the spring, a favorite activity was enjoying the University Concert Orchestra playing outdoor concerts in Mirror Lake Hollow.

Gregory thought he would go talk with the instructor whose name Chen had given him. If he decided not to take the course, no harm done. One morning, he walked across campus to the Department of East Asian Languages and Literatures, in the Enarson Classroom Building, to see if he could find Fong Li. She was listed on the office directory as L. Fong, so Gregory headed to her office. Li happened to be sitting in her office when Gregory walked in and introduced himself. She smiled and said, "You're the student Daniel Chen told me about. It's nice to meet you." She then asked, "What can I do for you?"

Ms. Fong was an extremely attractive women in her mid or late twenties. For a moment Gregory's mind wandered away from why he came to see her, but he quickly recovered. He told her he was interested is taking a class in Mandarin Chinese as an elective. She asked why he was interested in taking Chinese. He responded by indicating he thought learning some Chinese might be as important in the future as learning Spanish has been for a lot of Americans. She agreed and suggested he take Chinese 1101.01—Level One Chinese 1: Classroom Track. It is an introductory course to the Mandarin spoken and writing system. Li indicated she would be teaching the class next semester and would love to have Gregory in one of her classes. That sealed it for Gregory. He was already enamored with Li Fong or Fong Li, whatever her name was. She had a class to teach in a few minutes, so she gave him her teaching schedule for the next semester. Gregory headed back to the dorm, all the time thinking about being in class with Fong Li next year.

The rest of the school year seemed to go quickly for Gregory. Spring had been delightful and studying under one the big trees on the Oval was always pleasant. He had a good semester and was halfway through the pre-law program. His concern turned to a summer job to pay for next year. Last summer, he had worked as a logistics coordinator on the railroad. This summer, he hoped he could get another railroad job. The pay was good, and living at home, he could bank all his money for the fall. Fortunately, he did get another summer job on the railroad, making even more money. The summer was too short, but with what he had saved, it was back to Columbus for another year of school.

Gregory decided since he was taking the Mandarin Chinese course, he would only take fifteen hours this semester. He had enough credit hours to maintain his class standing and was on track to meet all graduation requirements. The dorm was still the best place to live. In the dorm, you have maid service to clean your room and change the sheets once a week, food service to provide your meals, and free transportation around campus. He settled in for his junior year. All his classes, except the Mandarin class, were in Fisher Hall.

He enjoyed the Mandarin course and especially being in Fong's class. The course was a little more difficult than he thought it would be. The homework was mostly learning to make alphabet characters, remembering the meaning of the Chinese characters, and listening to simple conversation. Gregory was glad Chen had given him a little head start. The A he received in the introductory course did not hurt either. It was a no brainer to take the follow-on course the next semester, again from Li. The yearlong academic relationship with her earned him two A's. Gregory did not see Chen on campus during the year, but he was more interested in seeing Li Fong than he was looking up Chen.

Gregory was starting to look ahead toward his senior year and applying to law school. While he was at home the previous summer, he talked with a friend who was in the Air National Guard (ANG) and then with a Guard Recruiter. He was told, if he enlisted in the ANG when he earned his undergraduate degree, he could apply for a Direct Commission as a Second Lieutenant. He could use the extra money, stay in law school, and attend Air Guard meetings one weekend a month. Therefore, Gregory enlisted in the ANG and spent the summer between his junior and senior years of undergraduate school at Lackland Air Force Base (AFB), Texas. He returned home just in time to go back to school. Fortunately, he had saved enough money from working on the railroad the two previous summers that he was able to get by for another year.

The courses his senior year were more difficult, but more interesting than most of those he had taken during his first three years at Ohio State. He did not take any more Chinese, but he did go by the Enarson Classroom Building to look up Li. She seemed pleased to see him. After his second or third visit to her office she finally invited Gregory to meet her at the China House for afternoon tea. It was his first visit to the house, and he was impressed with the Chinese decorations. There were only a few people there, but the tea was served ceremoniously. During the conversation, Gregory inquired about Daniel Chen. Li told her guest Chen had graduated at the end of three years and was in graduate school elsewhere, but she was uncertain where he was now. Li sensed that Gregory's interest in her was more than just in maintaining a friendship. When they were ready to finish tea, she suggested because of the age difference, Gregory should not expect to see her again. Besides, she was about to conclude her studies at Ohio State and would be moving on. Clearly, she was cutting it off. With his tail between his legs, he headed to the

Ohio Union for an early beer. He was now twenty-one and could buy beer in the Student Union.

He had been accepted to enter law school at Ohio State in September, so after graduating from the Fisher Business College, he headed back to Hamilton to work and replenish his bank account. However, this summer would be a little different. He had accepted a Direct Commission as a Second Lieutenant in the Ohio ANG and would have to serve two weeks at "summer camp." Since it was in the middle of the summer break from school, he was not able to get another job working for the railroad. Instead, he worked as a laborer on the loading dock for a prefab home builder in Hamilton.

The first two years of law school required a lot of work. Having the once-a-month weekend ANG drills was almost a pleasant distraction. As a second lieutenant in the Reserves, he was training to be an intelligence officer. His assignment was at the squadron level.

Gregory was in the second semester of his last year of law school and was still uncertain what he wanted to do after graduation. He had not yet started interviewing for jobs. He did not want to stay in Columbus, and he did not really want to go back to Hamilton. Doug thought about applying to the US Air Force for the Judge Advocates General's Corps (JAG), but they required him to resign his Air National Guard (and Air Force Reserve) Commissions before applying, without any guarantee of being accepted as a JAG officer. He decided against applying.

When it was announced the Federal Bureau of Investigation (FBI) would be at the law school, recruiting for positions as FBI special agents, he decided to attend. Two special agents from the Columbus Resident Agency (RA) spent over an hour explaining the opportunity to four law students. The employment requirements included being at least twenty-five years of age. However, Gregory would only be twenty-three when he graduated from law school, and when he asked about an age waiver, he was told no waivers were available.

After graduation from law school, Gregory stayed in Columbus to study for the Ohio bar examination. When the exam was over, while he waited for results, it was time for a short vacation and some time to just think about what was next. As an ANG officer and military reservist, he could fly space available on military aircraft anywhere in the United States. Flying out of Wright-Patterson AFB, in Dayton, Ohio, he headed for California. There he visited relatives and interviewed for a couple of jobs. Since he was not a resident of California, he could not take their bar exam for at least a year, and without passing the bar, he could not get a job practicing law. That was fine with him because he really did not want to go into private practice. While in California, he interviewed with the US Securities and Exchange Commission office in Hollywood. They told him his application would be sent to their headquarters in Washington,

DC, and he would be advised. With no real job prospects in California, it was time to return to Ohio to be sworn into the Ohio bar and to attend his ANG weekend meeting.

By the time Gregory returned to Ohio, all the good jobs in Columbus had been taken. The only legal job available was handling preliminary hearings in municipal court for the Legal Aid Society and supervising OSU senior law students working in clinic. It was not a career-enhancing job, but it provided a living while he decided what to do with his life.

Friday was usually a slow day. Gregory was done well before noon in municipal court, and there was no clinic on Friday afternoons, but since he was out early, he stopped into the clinic.

When he arrived, the clinic secretary who answered the phone said, "The FBI wants to speak to you.

Gregory wondered why on earth the FBI would call him, so he walked over to her desk and took the call. "Hello?"

"This is Danny Johnson, senior resident agent (SRA), in Columbus. Someone had indicated to us that you might be interested in the FBI."

Gregory confirmed he was interested, and Johnson suggested they get together to talk about it. Gregory was not busy right then and asked if Johnson was available anytime that afternoon. Their offices were only a short walk from each other, so twenty minutes later, Gregory was sitting in the Columbus Resident

Agency (RA). Johnson repeated much of what Gregory already knew from the presentation made at the law school. Finally, Gregory proffered he knew he was too young, having just turned twenty-four. Johnson assured him his age was not a problem and they could get a waiver on the age requirement. Gregory was then very interested. Johnson gave him the application paperwork and suggested Gregory drop it off at the RA when he had completed it.

Returning to his own office, with a couple of hours until quitting time, Gregory started in on the application and other papers. Since he had no girlfriends he could call and nothing planned for the weekend, he decided to work on the application. It took most of the weekend to complete, but by Sunday evening it was done. The next day, after court, he delivered the application papers to SA Johnson. Gregory was told the next step would be an interview with the special agent in charge (SAC) of the Cincinnati Division. The SAC was going to be in Columbus the following day, and Johnson wondered if Gregory was available.

After court on Tuesday, Gregory was sitting in front of SAC Ed Mason. The interview seemed uneventful to Gregory until they got to the minimum age requirements and a waiver. While Gregory was less than twelve months under the age requirement, he looked like he could pass for a sixteen-year-old—not good when you are trying to get an age waiver.

SAC Mason said, "We don't want people calling us up and asking if we are sending Boy Scouts to do the work of the FBI." At that moment Gregory thought the interview was over, but Mason stood up and said, "We have a new agents class starting this coming Monday. If I can get you in, will you go?"

Without hesitation Gregory said "Yes."

What had only months ago looked like a "no go" was now a "get it done yesterday" exercise.

Before leaving the RA, Johnson cornered Gregory and told him he would have to take a physical exam at nearby Lockbourne AFB, on Wednesday. Between court in the morning and clinic in the afternoon it would be difficult to work it into Gregory's schedule. Not a problem for the FBI to solve. The next morning Gregory was in the office of the Air Force flight surgeon at 4 a.m. for his physical, and by 9 a.m., he was in court. That afternoon, Gregory took the written exam in the RA.

Thursday was a routine day for Gregory—court in the morning and clinic in the afternoon. At lunch time, he did see a couple of the agents from the RA on the street in Columbus. They acknowledged him but did not speak to him. Gregory began feeling a little uneasy about his chances. In the afternoon his mother called him at his office and wanted to know what was going on. Gregory had not told his mom or anyone else about applying for a job as a Special Agent. She told Doug there were FBI Agents all over the neighborhood in Hamilton asking questions about him. She was relieved to find out why. When he arrived back at his apartment that evening there was a telegram from the FBI, Washington, DC, advising he had been appointed to be a special agent, and that if he accepted the position, he should report to the Bureau in Washington, DC, the following Monday morning.

The only people Gregory called were his landlord and his mother. There was no one else in his life he had to call. He told his landlord he would be vacating the furnished apartment on Saturday morning. Then he called his mother to say, "I will be home on Saturday afternoon and will fly to DC on Sunday." On Friday morning, he went to the office before going to court to give his resignation letter to his boss, who was not surprised. His boss had been interviewed by the FBI two days earlier, while Gregory was in court. Since there was no clinic on Friday afternoons, Gregory spent the afternoon packing up his world belongings, which were few. He was about to become an FBI agent.

➤➤ Chapter 2 ◄◄◄

G regory flew from Cincinnati to Reagan Airport, in
Washington, DC, on Sunday afternoon, checking
into the Hotel Harrington on Eleventh Street, near
the FBI building. On Monday morning, just one week
after being interviewed by Ed Mason, he was about to
become an FBI agent. Suitcase in hand, he walked to
the FBI Building on Pennsylvania Avenue. Checking
in at the visitor's center in the lobby, as nobody walks
around anywhere in the FBI building without a visible
pass or an escort, he was escorted to a classroom on one
of the upper floors. There were already a few candidates
in the room. Over the next fifteen minutes the rest of
the class arrived. The class appeared to be about twenty-
four people.

Promptly, at the appointed time, the assistant
director (AD) of the Human Resources Division arrived
and introduced himself. After a very short welcome, the
AD introduced the group to their class counselor and
then left. The class counselor then addressed the class
about what they would be doing the rest of the day. The
morning would be devoted to taking the oath of office;
completing personnel forms, including insurance; and
personal interviews. After lunch, they would be called

out for polygraph testing, foreign language testing, and briefing on their training at the FBI academy in Quantico, Virginia. At 3 o'clock, the class would board a Bureau bus for the trip to Quantico. After dinner at the Academy, they would receive their room assignments and instructions for the following day.

After the class had taken the oath of office, and about an hour into the morning session, Gregory was the first new agent summoned for an interview. An escort took him to a small conference room in the Behavioral Science Section. There he met a man who introduced himself as Doc Watson.

After just a minute of idle chatter Watson told Gregory, "You have been targeted by the Chinese government. Do you have any idea why?"

Gregory said, "I don't have a clue, but it must have something to do with my taking the Mandarin language courses." Doc Watson then continued to ask Gregory about why he took a Chinese course in undergraduate school and what contact he has had with anyone who is Chinese? Gregory related meeting Daniel Chen in freshman English class and taking two semesters of Mandarin from Li Fong. The questions went into great detail about Gregory's relationship with these two people, including wanting to know if he had any kind of sexual relationship with either. He had not. The interview lasted over an hour. Next, Gregory was escorted to a testing center where he took the foreign language ability test and then a test of his Mandarin knowledge and skills. They did not ask him to take a test in Spanish.

By then, it was lunch time. Another escort walked him to the men's room and then the cafeteria. There were a lot of people having lunch, but Gregory did not recognize any of the people from the new agents group. Maybe they were there or maybe not. None of them had had an opportunity earlier to introduce themselves to each other. The escort stayed with him through lunch. When he was finished, Gregory was escorted to a room for polygraphing. The special agent conducting the polygraph test had a couple of hours to review the interview with Doc Watson, and he seem to know as much about Gregory as he probably knew about himself. When the polygraph was over, it was getting close to the time to catch the bus to Quantico, and Gregory had not finished his employment paperwork.

Instead of going back to the classroom, his next escort took him to a meeting room where he was greeted by a deputy assistant director from Human Resources. He was told he would not be taking the bus to Quantico that afternoon, and instead they wanted him to spend the next day here at the seat of government (SOG) for more interviews. Gregory was beginning to have an uneasy feeling there was a problem with the Chinese issue but really did not understand why. After the meeting, he completed the employment paperwork, and they brought his luggage to him. Instead of taking the bus to Quantico he went back to the Hotel Harrington for the night. After such a long day, he was exhausted. Dinner in the hotel and a bottle of beer was all he could handle.

The next morning at 8 a.m., with suitcase in hand, he reported again to the FBI visitor's center. An escort took Gregory to an office where he was met by the HR deputy assistant director, and SA Lou "Woody" Woodward. Much to his surprise, instead of telling him they had a problem, they told him the FBI wanted to do something different with him. He would still be going through new agents training like he had planned, but he was not going to Quantico on the bus just yet. The reason for singling him out was because he was being targeted by the Chinese for possible recruitment. The FBI believed Gregory was "clean," and the Bureau wanted to use him undercover, if the opportunity presented itself. Gregory really did not know what to expect, but he had signed on to be an FBI agent, and he was ready to accept the challenge.

SA Woodward then briefed him on the details. Gregory would not be going to Quantico until the next new agents class, which was not for another couple of weeks. Since he did not know anyone in the class he met with the previous day, the Bureau was going to change his identity. He would be given a pseudonym for now, so the Chinese intelligence people did not find out he had become an FBI agent. The FBI would maintain a fake dossier for him under his real name. If the Chinese tried to contact him, the FBI could still bring him back, and there would be no record of Douglas Gregory having worked for the FBI. The time between now and the next new agents class would be spent learning his false identity, studying about Chinese culture, and brushing up on his Mandarin. Following his training at Quantico, he would be sent to the Defense Language Institute Foreign Language Center (DLIFLC), in Monterey, California, to take a Mandarin course. Throughout his time in language school, he would use the fake name. After language school, he would be assigned to one of the field offices where the FBI worked cases involving Chinese subjects and issues.

For the next two weeks, Gregory lived in an FBI safe house in Arlington, Virginia. During his time there, he read hundreds of pages of books and magazines about China, Chinese history, and their culture. He watched videos about China and even some Chinese movies. He listened to Chinese audio tapes and occasionally went to local Chinese restaurants to practice his Mandarin. A week into his stay, Woody showed up with a new driver's license and other identifying documents, all back dated, identifying him as Robert Charles Allen. Woody even had credit cards issued to Allen. Gregory gave his Ohio driver's license and credit cards to Woody in exchange for the new identification cards. From that point on, Gregory was to use his new name and to learn about R. C. "Bob" Allen from a detailed dossier the Bureau prepared. All that was left now was to start new agents class.

When the next group of new agents reported for class, Bob Allen showed up at the FBI visitor's center and was escorted to the same classroom where he reported earlier. This time, there seemed to be larger number of new agents. When he was asked to sign in on the register, he had to be careful to sign "Robert C. Allen" and not his real name, like he did a month earlier. At exactly 8:30, the assistant director of HR walked in and introduced himself to the class. After the same welcoming remarks he made to the previous class, the AD introduced the class counselor. They went through the same routine as the class had done earlier. This time, when Allen was called from class for his personal interview, he was taken to Woody's office instead of to Doc Watson's. It was more of a "how did it go" meeting that did not last long. They did not make him take the foreign language tests again. Instead, he was escorted back to the classroom to complete his employment paperwork under the name Robert C. Allen. After lunch in the cafeteria, he was called out again for another polygraph. This time, it was a different operator giving the test. Some of the questions were the same, but this time, the test included questions about his identity. Woody had instructed him to answer questions this time as Robert C. Allen so they could see how he would react if ever questioned about who he was.

At 3 o'clock, the class was loaded into buses for the trip to Quantico. The streets of Washington, DC, were already full of traffic, but the drivers knew how to deal with it, and within minutes, they were on the Shirley Highway headed south. During the trip, the new agents had their first chance to introduce themselves to each other. Bob Allen had to concentrate on where he was from and what he did before applying to be an FBI agent. It was not easy, so he elected not to say too much. It made for a quiet ride. When they arrived at the FBI Academy, they were instructed to leave their suitcases in the lobby. They were taken to the dining room for dinner, where they were already late. The rest of the students at the Academy had already eaten and had retired for the evening to their studies. After dinner, the new agents were given their room assignments. It had been a long day, so most just called it quits and turned in. Breakfast was at 6 a.m. and class was at 8.

The next morning, the first subject for new agent class was a briefing on what was expected personally from an FBI agent. "Always be a gentleman (or gentlewoman), dress for success, and never drink on duty." Special agents are expected to be a cut above everyone else. "Always seek to find the truth no matter whether if it will lead to someone going to jail or being exonerated from an allegation of a serious crime."

The training at the Academy was full of academic study about the Constitution, statutory law, FBI jurisdiction and the history of the Bureau. It was like three years of law school compacted into just a short period of time. There was also plenty of time on the firing range, personal security training, and a field trip to the FBI laboratory.

After thirteen weeks at the FBI Academy, it was time to graduate and move on to their first assignment. FBI Director James Comey was there, as were several other Bureau officials, and wives and family of members of the married agents. Bob Allen did not have any visitors for graduation. The graduating special agents were issued their official credentials, and then the ceremony was over just before noon. Most stayed for lunch, one last time. The only other thing to do that day, before leaving, was to go by the gun vault and pick up their government-issued .40 caliber Glock pistol. With a gun on their hips and credentials in their pockets, they were sent on their way to their next assignment.

→→ Chapter 3 ←←

Bob had five travel days to get to California. He had only briefly talked to his mother so she would not discuss his becoming an FBI agent. Now he needed to fly home for the weekend and fill in the blanks for her, as best he could. He could make no side trips to Columbus or attempts to contact any of his old friends. After a couple of days in Hamilton, he flew to San Francisco. Remaining overnight there, he caught the Friday afternoon Amtrack to Monterey. Allen checked into the Navy Lodge and, in the evening, went into town to survey the area.

Asking the cab driver to recommend a good restaurant, he was dropped off at a popular local eatery. As he entered, he noticed it was crowded, the sign of a good place to eat or drink. It had a bar area where people were dining. There was an open seat at the bar, and the hostess told Bob he could eat at the bar if he desired. He took the seat.

When he entered the bar, he did not go unnoticed. In keeping with his FBI agent image, he was "dressed to the nines" in a smart blue blazer and gray slacks. Most of the other men in the bar were dressed in what might be referred as Friday night casual. The women in the bar were better dressed than the men, and his seat at the bar was next to two very attractive women in their mid-twenties. They were obviously together. Bob ordered a beer and asked for a menu.

Perusing the menu, he asked the blonde sitting next to him, "Are you two regulars here?" She indicated they had been here a number of times. He then asked about the food and if they had any recommendations. The red head suggested everything was good, but the seafood was their specialty. Bob decided to start with an order of calamari.

"I take it you haven't been here before," responded the blonde.

Bob said, "I just arrived in Monterey to start school at the Persidio." The ice had been broken. Apparently, he was not the first student from the school they had encountered, but he looked younger than most of the other students at the school. "My name is Bob Allen."

The blonde responded, "I'm Shirley, and this is my friend Blair. We live in San Jose but come down here for a change of scenery." Bob indicated this was his first visit to Monterey and was looking forward to seeing the area. The girls had finished their drinks and decided to order some food at the bar, so the conversation continued for another hour. Shirley Hare and Blair Reed both work for Google in Mountain View.

They asked where he was from. Not wanting to say he was from Ohio, he responded, "I just moved here from Quantico, Virginia." At first, they figured he was a young naval officer, but now thought he must be a Marine. The conversation never got around to the fact he was an FBI agent.

"It has been a long travel day for me. I think I better get back to the hotel." Bob did not have any business cards, so he wrote his name and cell phone number on a napkin and handed it to Shirley, saying he hoped he would see them again. The girls decided they had enough, too, and offered to drop him off at the hotel where he was staying. He eagerly accepted the offer. Shirley's car was a two-door sedan. Bob climbed into the back seat for the ride. When they got to the hotel, he thanked them both, and said he hoped to see them again. They had not given him their telephone numbers, so he doubted he would ever hear from either one of them.

Bob spent Saturday morning running and exercising, and then spent the afternoon shopping for a car. After dinner in the hotel, he went over the welcoming materials given to him when he checked in the previous evening. He found a church to go to on Sunday morning and relaxed in the afternoon. He had adjusted to the time zone change and was ready to go on Monday morning.

Class was at 0800. As the students arrived they introduced themselves to each other. There were only six of them: five men and one woman. The female was a naval officer and was wearing her uniform on the first day of class. The men were dressed in suits or sport coats. This was not an ordinary college class. The class instructor was Dr. Luen Young. After she introduced herself to the class, she admonished, "While you know what your own limitations are in discussing yourselves with each other, you are prohibited from discussing with anyone outside the class who the class members are or who they work for." Bob had already sized up the members of the class. All were a little older than Bob. The naval officer, LCDR Margaret Cassidy, was a very attractive thirty-something woman. Bob decided of the rest, one was probably from the State Department, two were likely from the CIA, and the other was from some other government agency, probably the National Security Agency (NSA). Bob nicknamed the two students from the CIA as Spooky 1 and Spooky 2. A couple of the students had some exposure to Chinese, but none were native speakers.

The six-month-long class was different than the Mandarin classes "Bob" had taken in college. For this course, spouses who accompanied class members could participate in the course and class events, if they understood the rule about not identifying class members to those not part of the class. The Navy officer was married but unaccompanied. Bob was the only single member of the class. The other four had their wives with them, all eager to participate. Most of the time they had ten students in class. Monday through Friday was spent together, learning to speak and understand Mandarin, how to make and read Mandarin characters, and practicing pronunciation on each other. They also learned how to recognize when someone was speaking

Cantonese instead of Mandarin. Dr. Young was with the class during most of the day. They became their own little Chinese community. Occasionally they would go out together to a Chinese restaurant. On weekends, they would sometimes get together for a Chinese theme party. They had become a close-knit group.

Two weeks into class, Bob got a call on his cell phone from Shirley Hare. The first couple of weeks had been too busy for him to give much thought to whether Shirley or Blair might call him, but he perked up at the sound of her voice. After a few minutes of "How is it going" type chit chat, Shirley said, "There is an office get together next Saturday night. If you are available and interested, I would like you to go with me. It might be a fun evening."

Bob was past ready for an evening out with a pretty girl. He said he would, but he had to check to make sure he had no school conflicts that weekend. He verified her telephone number and said he would call her back the next evening. For a while that evening Bob's mind wandered from his studies. Bob's class had nothing scheduled on Saturday night, so when he called her back, he said he would enjoy going to her office party. He had leased a car for six months. All he needed was an address and what time to pick her up.

On Saturday, Bob drove to San Jose, picked up Shirley at her apartment, and drove to East Palo Alto. Luckily, the party was not on the Google property in Mountain View where, because he was carrying, security might require him to identify himself as an FBI agent. Instead, the party was at the Four Seasons Hotel. It was a glorious event with a couple of hundred people in attendance. It was an eclectic group of people from various nationalities, and everyone seemed to know everyone else, except Shirley's date. Blair Reed was there, constantly surrounded by an entourage of young men. Shirley hung on Bob's arm through most of the evening, introducing him only by his name. It suddenly occurred to her she really didn't know anything about him, except he was a student at the Persidio.

During the evening while dancing with Bob, Shirley happened to put her left hand on his hip. Bob is right-handed so what she felt was his Glock. At that moment, a million thoughts probably went through her mind. She realized what she was touching, and she knew he was not a criminal or else he would not be at the Persidio, but why would a military officer be carrying a gun?

She asked him, "Is there something I should know?" Bob smiled at her and told her there was, but it would have to wait until they left the party.

On the way back to San Jose, Bob finally told Shirley what she had forgotten to ask when they first met. "I am carrying because I'm an FBI agent, and I am required to carry it when I am on duty. I am on duty 24/7, except when I am sleeping or in the shower." She was relieved.

When they got back to her apartment, it was too late to invite him in, but the evening did end with a passionate kiss and a promise from Bob to call her.

Shirley was a slender, very attractive blonde with an easy personality. Over the next several weekends, they met several times for Saturday or Sunday lunch in the Silicon Valley area, but some weekend evenings were reserved for his class "Chinese community" affairs. He did get permission from Dr. Young and the remainder of the students in the class to invite Shirley to one of their dinners out. This was her first inkling Bob was studying Chinese. Shirley was told not to ask questions about where anyone was from or what they did, and she agreed. It all went well.

Over Christmas, the school was closed for the holidays, so Bob flew back to Ohio to be with his aging mother. For about nine days, Bob morphed into Douglas Gregory again. No need to confuse her with his cover name and story. As far as she knew he was just taking more graduate courses in California. No mention of the FBI was made, and his mother seemed to have forgotten he even applied to the Bureau to be a special agent. He made no attempt to see any former friends. When his vacation was over, he flew back to California. The holiday was uneventful.

When Bob got back to Monterey, he called Shirley to set up a date. She told him a group from work was planning a ski weekend in late January or early February to Lake Tahoe, and she wanted to invite him to join her. Bob was not a skier, but it was something had always wanted to do. This was his opportunity.

"I'll need to take lessons," he confessed.

She indicated it was not a problem because it had been a while since she skied and would probably need to take a class too. She related, "Some of the people on the trip won't even do doing any skiing. They just go for the atmosphere and the restaurants." He told her to let him know the details so he could check it against the school schedule.

Back in school everyone seemed excited by the fact they were halfway through the course. They all seemed to pick up where they left off in December. There were no slackers in this class. Commander Cassidy seemed a little stressed after the holiday break. Bob picked up on it and invited her to have a drink with him after class. Apparently, she had visited her husband in Japan over the holidays, and it did not go particularly well. Her husband is a Navy pilot, flying reconnaissance off the Russian coast. Even though Bob was four or five years younger than Margaret, he became her sounding board and best friend.

The Google ski trip was scheduled for the three-day President's Day weekend in February, which was perfect timing. When he was talking to Shirley about room reservations, she indicated the extra expense for two rooms was not necessary. They could share a room. He said he did not sleep well on a sofa and suggested she reserve a two-bedroom accommodation. He would pick up the extra cost. She did not push it. The plan was to drive from Silicon Valley on Friday afternoon. It is about a three-hour drive over I-80. Since snow in the mountains could be a problem, Shirley had arranged a ride for them with an office friend who had a four-wheel-drive vehicle with snow tires. All Bob needed to do was buy himself some ski clothes. Everything else he needed could be bought or rented in Lake Tahoe.

When the time came for the ski weekend, Bob ~~was~~ took annual leave on Friday. Monday was the holiday. He drove to San Jose in the morning, and that afternoon, they packed themselves into the friend's SUV. In the wintertime, it gets dark early in the mountains, and they arrived at the lodge as the evening was setting in. They checked in and decided to have a drink and dinner at the lodge. It had been a long day. A couple of hours later, they were exhausted and decided it was time to retire. Tomorrow would be a big day on the slopes.

Since Bob had suggested Shirley reserve a two-bedroom accommodation, it was clear he was playing it straight with her. She did not contest or comment on his decision. After a passionate goodnight kiss, each retired to their own room. Twenty minutes later, Bob was in bed and sound asleep. During the night someone slipped into bed beside him. She was naked and he could tell it was Shirley from the perfume she wore. She was soft, warm, and cuddly. He rolled over and kissed her, saying only "I am glad you are here."

The following morning, Shirley returned to her room, and they got dressed for a morning of skiing. After an early breakfast, they shuttled to the ski school area to rent skis and boots, and to sign up for some lessons. Several people from their group were also there, including Blair. Since he was a beginner, Bob opted for a half-day private lesson. Shirley and Blair had both skied before, so they signed up for a beginner's level group lesson. All agreed to meet at the bottom of the slope after the lesson and have lunch together. Bob was athletic, so he took to the skiing rather well. His instructor kept him on the easy blue slopes so he would not get into trouble. He had a couple of falls, but nothing a beginner would not normally expect to have. It was an exciting experience for him, and he was looking forward to the next day. As planned, after the lesson, he met Shirley and Blair. They secured their skis and boots in a rental locker, and it was off to lunch.

Lunch discussion was about their ski experiences, but Bob could sense Shirley and Blair had talked about what had happened last night. Shirley seemed to have a glow about her, and Blair seemed eager to know more about Bob. After lunch, they shuttled back to the lodge for an afternoon of relaxation. Some of the skiers in the group stayed on the slopes all day, but a number gathered back at the lodge to sit around the fireplace in the lobby and visit. Shirley introduced Bob to several of her fellow workers, and when asked, he admitted he worked for the FBI and that he was a student at the Persidio. He had not talked to Shirley about Blair, but in the course of the afternoon, he learned she was Dr. Blair Reed, senior assistant to the director of training and development at the company. The rest of the conversation was mainly about where everyone was going to eat that evening and who was going to ski with whom the next day. Shirley had purchased a half-day group lesson for two days, and Bob did not think he was ready to join a large group. He said he would take another private lesson on Saturday. Blair indicated she was still in a little over her head in the group lesson and asked Bob if he would be agreeable to taking a semi-private lesson with her. He looked at Shirley, and she seemed not to have a problem with it, so it was all set. After an exquisite dinner that evening with a small group of people from the office, everyone was exhausted. When Bob and Shirley retired to their room, there was no pretense about sleeping in separate beds.

On Sunday morning after breakfast, it was off to the slopes again. After picking up their boots and skis, they were off to the ski school area. Shirley joined her group. Blair and Bob signed up for a half-day, semi-private lesson. Blair was more advanced than Bob, but he kept up with her and the instructor. He was gaining more confidence and enjoyed the session. Like before, after the lesson, they met Shirley at the bottom of the slope, secured their ski equipment for the night, and headed back to the lodge. It had been another enjoyable morning. The crowd in the lodge was a little bigger than the day before. Couples seemed to come and go all afternoon. Bob noticed at times they seemed to disappear with different partners than he thought they were with. He mentioned this to Shirley and was told there are some couples who like to mix their skiing and their sex partners on these getaway weekends. In the evening, it was off to dinner again, this time with Blair and her date. Bob did not know if Blair was staying with her companion but decided not to ask. He did not need to know. He was more concerned with protecting Shirley's reputation.

Monday morning was their last day, so the three of them opted not to take another lesson and instead to ski together. Shirley was the best skier in the group, but she kept them on the blue trails. There were no serious falls or accidents. All in all, it was the perfect ending of a fabulous weekend. When it was over, they turned in their boots and skis and headed back to the lodge for lunch. The plan was to leave in the early afternoon so they could get home before dark. After lunch, they piled into the SUV with the couple they came with and headed for San Jose. Luckily, the weather had been good most of the weekend, and they encountered no snow problem going home. They picked up some fast food before they got to Shirley's. Bob and Shirley ate in her apartment. It had been another long day and an even longer weekend, so it seemed. Shirley talked about getting back to work the next day, so Bob excused himself and headed back to Monterey.

On Tuesday morning, after the holiday, everyone was eager to get back to school. There were only a few weeks left before they finished. Most of the students were anxious to take on their next assignment. Bob still did not know where his transfer would take him, but during the lunch hour, he got a call from a cell phone in Washington, DC.

When Bob answered the called the caller said, "Good afternoon Bob. This is Woody. How is it going?" Bob told him it has been going well and everything was good.

Woody replied, "I have two things I want to talk about, if you have a minute." He did, so he told Woody to go ahead.

"We have had someone checking on your friend from Hamilton. Have you heard from anyone about him, or do you have any ideas why?" Bob told him he had not heard anything about his friend, and nothing had transpired to give Bob any clue why someone would be checking on Doug. Woody indicated not to worry; they had it covered.

Woody then told Bob, "Just wanted to give you a head's up. Your transfer orders, for after school, will be issued shortly. Your first office assignment will be in San Francisco. Your reporting date will be on Monday following the Friday you finish school, but you have some accrued leave, so if you want to take a short vacation, let me know. I can put you on annual leave for a week."

Bob thanked him for the advance information and indicated he would think about some time off. He would let Woody know.

Bob's mind was somewhere else all afternoon as he pondered his first office assignment. After class, Margaret Cassidy invited Bob to have drink with her, and they adjourned to a quiet local watering hole. She was still awaiting her next assignment, but she had talked to her husband over the long weekend, and he told her he was filing for a divorce. Not sure how he could help her, Bob just listened. After a few drinks he suggested they have dinner together. After dinner, he dropped her at her quarters. He was surprised when she kissed him on the lips that he attributed to too many drinks.

When Bob got back to his hotel, he called Shirley to see how she survived the ski trip and to tell her he would be moving to San Francisco in mid-March. She was elated he would still be in the area. He told her he had some vacation time coming and was thinking about taking a week in Hawaii. Did she want to go with him?

The next few weeks went fast. Since he would be staying in California, he decided to renew the lease on his automobile. He was in a good position to take a week off before reporting and still be able to get settled in San Francisco. Bob used some of the remaining school weekends to look for a furnished apartment in San Francisco. At one time, Margaret had been stationed at the Alameda Naval Air Station across the bay from San Francisco and volunteered to help and give advice. With some additional help from the FBI office in San Francisco, he began his search. Bob and Margaret made several weekend day trips to "the City by the Bay" before he found something, which was acceptable and which he could afford.

Bob told Margaret about his plan to take a vacation in Hawaii before reporting to work. He had never been there. She said she was stationed there, too, at one time, and because she had some leave time coming, she would glad to be his tour guide. This was getting too serious. She was a married woman, and he knew the Bureau would not approve of his being involved with her. Rather than tell her he had invited Shirley to go with him, he explained that the Bureau rules prohibited it. Margaret was disappointed, but she seemed to understand. She asked if they could stay in touch after Mandarin school and remain friends. Bob did not see a problem with staying in contact with a former classmate.

The Mandarin course was coming to an end. Shirley had agreed to go to Hawaii with him. When the class finished the course, there was a small mid-morning ceremony. Nothing elaborate. The students and wives who participated were given certificates of completion. They exchanged hugs all around, and off they went into the Chinese Year of the Rooster. Bob drove to San Jose, picked up Shirley, and off they went to the SFO Airport. Next stop, Oahu.

⇒⇒ Chapter 4 ⇐⇐

The flight back from Hawaii ran late, so they opted to spend the night in Bob's apartment. There were lots they could do on a Friday night in San Fran, but they were both exhausted from the week's activities. After a week of eating in restaurants, they decided to stay home and eat in. On Saturday, Bob drove Shirley back to San Jose. After a somewhat emotional goodbye, Bob returned to his apartment to prepare himself for his first "real" day on the job.

On Sunday, Bob sought out a local church and went to the late service. The afternoon was spent mostly relaxing, and it gave him an opportunity to meet some of his neighbors. Then late Sunday, he had a conversation with Shirley. The first day would be an early start, so Bob turned in before his usual bedtime.

Bob appeared at the FBI office the following morning at 7 a.m. A security receptionist was on duty, so Bob gave her his credentials and announced he was a new agent reporting for duty. The receptionist told him they were expecting him, and she gave him the register to sign. He was asked to have a seat and an assistant special agent-in-charge would be with him momentarily. Within a couple of minutes, ASAC F. L.

Furginson appeared, introduced himself, and handed Bob's credentials back to him.

Furginson said, "Come on in and let me introduce you to some of the people you will be working with." They retired to the ASAC's office.

Furginson said he noticed Bob's profile was unusual in that normally agents do not get a chance to attend language school until they have been in the field for at least three years. He was curious why Bob got to go to Monterey before his first office assignment.

Bob shrugged it off saying," I don't know. Maybe they just needed more Mandarin speakers." It was obvious the ASAC was not aware the person he was talking to had been targeted by the Chinese before he became an agent. Bob suspected he probably did not know Bob Allen was a cover name either. He decided to just be unknowing and leave well enough alone. For now, he was Special Agent Robert C. Allen.

During the discussion, SA Ted Lu entered the office. Furginson introduced Bob to Lu and said, "Ted is on the squad you are assigned to. He will show you around the office, introduce you to the other members of the squad, and work with you for a couple of weeks while you learn the ropes."

After taking Bob to the HR section to be photographed for a building pass, Ted took Bob on a tour of the office. He was shown his cubical in the area where his squad worked, the gun vault where firearms were kept, the cafeteria, and special areas of the office, which required a special-access pass. Bob would have access to the areas involving the kind of work he would be doing. Because of Bob's Mandarin skills and training, he was assigned to what was known internally as the "Red Dragon Squad." Lu told him that while they handled some criminal cases, when the subjects spoke only Chinese, their primary function was to gather domestic intelligence on activities of Chinese nationals living and working here and on Chinese spy activities. He reminded Bob of some of the special handling rules he learned at Quantico for counter-intelligence matters. During the morning, Bob met a few of the agents on his squad, but most had already left the office to work their leads. He would meet the rest of them later.

Lu suggested they hit Chinatown and have some lunch. It was only a short walk from the FBI office to Chinatown. On the way, Lu gave Bob his first lesson in intelligence gathering. "Once we walk around Chinatown, every shop keeper and restaurant staff worker will know you are an FBI agent. That is good because if someone wants to contact us, they will recognize who you are. You wouldn't make a good undercover person anyway because you do not look like us. The Chinese are very clannish. What they won't know is whether or not you speak their language and can understand what they are talking about if you overhear them." He added, "When you are talking to anyone in public, always speak in English. Only speak in Mandarin when you are talking to someone you know doesn't speak English and then only in private. Now let's go introduce you to the Chinese community."

Lu selected a small, but popular, family-owned restaurant on Grant Avenue. The food was good, and while they dined, the discussion was about how Bob was enjoying San Francisco and whether he had been to Chinatown or to Fisherman's Wharf before. The conversation was strictly vanilla, but everyone recognized Special Agent Lu and his new associate. The word would spread fast. On the way back to the office, Bob and Lu talked about office politics and what to do if Bob needed something. Back in the office, Bob met a couple of the other agents on the Red Dragon Squad and talked about what they would be doing until some cases were assigned to Bob.

Over the next several weeks, Bob and Lu worked leads in San Francisco and the surrounding communities. Once it was apparent Bob knew his way around the office and the city, the ASAC began assigning him leads and cases. The first was a crime on the high seas matter, aboard a Chinese freighter which was currently in the San Francisco port. The ship had previously docked in Long Beach, California, so the Los Angeles Field Office was the office of origin (OO:) for the case. Bob was assigned leads to cover. He set out to interview the captain of the vessel and any crew members who were on board when the crime happened. Bob remembered the advice about when to speak English and when to speak Chinese. The captain spoke good English, but some of the crew members spoke no English. While there were only a half dozen people to interview, it took most of the day. Bob then returned to the office to review his notes and prepare the FD 302s. He had now completed his first solo task as a special agent.

A couple of months after Bob was assigned to the SF office, all hell broke loose with what were known as the Russia–Russia Collusion Hoax and the Crossfire Hurricane Scandals. There was an increase in the information from Mainland China about the scandals in the US. It did not appear on the surface the Chinese government was directly involved, but it was clear they were attempting to take advantage of the president's precarious political situation. The scandals did not directly impact the work in the SF Office. Director Comey was fired, and the Bureau got a new director, Christopher Wray. Political turmoil, even in a government organization like the FBI, can cause a lot of consternation. Transfers of personnel usually follow any major change of leadership at the seat of government. Bob was not worried about being transferred somewhere else, but he did not want to lose his mentors. The ASACs and agents seeking advancement are always vulnerable.

Over the next few months, several new cases and more leads were assigned to him. During the course of the work he was doing, Bob was made aware of the need to develop sources in the Chinese community who could provide information about Chinese nationals and any kind of illegal activity. His first opportunity to do this happened early one Sunday morning when Bob was driving his leased car to the Palace of the Fine Arts area, near the Golden Gate Bridge, where he planned to run and exercise. While sitting at a stop sign, he was rear-ended by a young Asian man, Chen Fang. No one appeared to be injured, and the damage was not great, so they exchanged insurance information and went on their ways. Bob later realized he would have to report this accident to the Bureau, so that afternoon he went to the home of Fang to get more information. Bob explained he wanted to make sure the young man had not suffered any injuries. Also, he needed some additional information to file a required report of the accident with his employer. The driver was surprised when he found out he had run into an FBI agent.

As the conversation with the young driver developed, Chen told Bob he worked for an old Chinese man who owned an import–export business. He related the old man was constantly surrounded by other old Chinese men. Some were citizens, and some were Chinese permanent resident aliens who had lived here for years but never took citizenship. They would spend most of their time in the store just talking and playing Xiangqi or Mahjong, while Chen handled the business of the store. The old men talked a lot about China and world events involving the Chinese leadership, and they seemed to be well informed about what was going on in China. They were very much pro-China. Chen did not care for this since he was born here in the US. He loved his country. Bob suggested Chen keep his ear to the ground, and if he heard anything interesting to give him a call. Chen said he would.

Bob was keeping busy with work. FBI Agents are on duty 24/7 and work long hours. You never know when something important will happen. Weekends can frequently be interrupted by duty. It was better for Shirley to come to San Francisco for the weekends than for Bob to go to San Jose, and she did. Bob began to think in terms of a permanent relationship, but how does someone with a fake name get married? The relationship with Shirley continued well into 2018.

After the weekend with Shirley, it was back to work for Bob. His mind wandered for a while, but by lunch time, he was fully mentally involved in his work. He had a couple of leads to follow up on in the city and a bunch of paperwork to catch up on in the office. He left the office at 5 o'clock to have a drink at a "watering hole" near the office and maybe a bite to eat before going back to his apartment. About an hour later, his cell phone rang. It was Chen Fang, the young driver who had run into him a few weeks earlier.

He answered, "Hi, this is Bob Allen."

The reply, "This is Chen, do you remember me?"

"Sure do. What's happening?"

Chen then said, "I think I have some information you might be interested in."

Bob cut him off. "Best not talk about it on the telephone. When is a good time to meet?"

Bob had nothing planned for the evening, except to eat. Chen had finished at work for the rest of the day. So, they planned to meet in a fast-food restaurant not far from where Chen lived. Bob instructed Chen to order some food and to sit at a bar counter, to keep a seat next to him empty, and not to speak to Bob until he spoke first. This was to make sure Chen was not compromised.

When Bob arrived, Chen was already sitting in a counter seat with an empty stool next to him. Bob ordered his food, looked around the room like he was looking for a place to sit. He took the stool next to Chen. Neither one spoke.

About five minutes into his meal, without looking at Chen, Bob asked," Do you recognize anyone in here other than me?"

Chen indicated he did not.

Bob then asked, "Do you remember the car I was driving?" Chen said he did.

"I am parked across the parking lot. When you finish your meal, leave and go to my car. It is unlocked. Get into the driver's seat and wait for me."

When he had finished eating, Chen left the restaurant and headed to Bob's car. Bob stayed behind in the restaurant and watched to see if anyone followed Chen out the door. No one seemed to notice Chen leaving. A few minutes later, Bob finished his meal, dumped his trash in the container at the door, and then went out outside. He stood by the door to see if anyone else was exiting. No one did, so Bob headed to his car and slid into the passenger side. He told Chen to watch the restaurant door for a couple of minutes to make sure no one was interested in their meeting.

When it appeared all was clear, Bob asked about what was happening. Chen related he had overheard a conversation of the group of old men where he worked. They were talking about the niece of one of the Chinese nationals who either works in the office of one of the Bay Area congressmen or is his girlfriend. Chen was not absolutely sure of their relationship, but heard the old men talk about her passing information she gets from the congressman to the people in the Chinese consulate in San Francisco. She apparently came here on a student visa. Her name is Christine Fang. Bob did not recognize the name of the congressman but thanked Chen for the information and asked him to stay in touch if he came up with anything else. He told Chen to go back into the restaurant, use the restroom, and then buy himself a drink or something before leaving. Bob would stay in his car for a while to see if Chen was being followed. Chen did exactly what he was told. Apparently, there was no tail on Chen, so Bob called it a day. He took a circuitous way home to make sure he was not followed either.

The next morning, Bob went to see ASAC Furginson and to relate what happened the evening before. The ASAC told Bob that the congressman was a Democrat representative from across the Bay in Alameda. After listening to the background about how Bob came to find Chen, and his work situation, Furginson suggest they open a security informant (SI) file on Chen and pass his information on to the Bureau. The Bureau is the OO: for all security cases, so they will let the field office know what they want done, if anything. Bob now had his first SI.

There was no immediate response from the SOG about the Chinese woman connected to the congressman. Bob kept busy on other assigned counter-intelligence matters. Sometimes he would lunch on Stockton Street or Grant Avenue. Occasionally he had to interview people who worked in Chinatown. A few regulars in the area acknowledged and greeted him, but nobody ever approached him with any issues, which would be of interest to the FBI.

In March, Bob celebrated is first year in the field. He received an excellent review from his supervisor. No longer considered a rookie, he was a full-fledged part of the squad. To celebrate, he, Ted Lu, and some of the other agents from the Red Dragons went out after work for a drink. One of the agents gave Bob a Red Dragon lapel pin, but he was not to wear it in the office or in public. It was just a recognition of his acceptance by his peers.

→→ Chapter 5 ←←

Weekends with Shirley became a regular thing. Bob continued to think seriously about his situation with her. Turns out, it was not something he had to think about much longer. Shirley told Bob she was leaving her position at Google in Mountain View and moving back to Texas to take care of her elderly parents. She had no choice. Besides, several Big Tech companies were developing facilities in Austin, and she was sure she could get a good position with one of them. Bob was stunned but understood. He had become attached to her but marrying Shirley would not solve her problem. Duty calls! She had a duty to perform in Texas, and he still had a duty to carry out with the FBI. Sunday was a difficult day for both.

Sometime after she had been gone for a while, Bob tried to call Shirley to see how she was doing. Her cell phone number had been disconnected. It was strange he had not heard from her. He assumed her old cell either belonged to Google or maybe she just decided to get a new number in Texas. Finally, he decided to called Blair at Google. He got her voice mail. That evening, he got a call back from Blair. Instead of going right to the subject about how Shirley was doing or giving him a new phone number for her, Blair said, "I am coming to San Francisco the day after tomorrow for a two-day meeting at the Four Seasons Embarcadero. Can we meet for a drink?"

Bob told her sure. After agreeing to a time to meet her at the hotel she said, "I've got to go. Very busy. Will see you Friday." She was gone. A strange conversation, but he would find out more when he saw her.

After work on Friday, Bob headed to the Four Seasons Hotel. He found a comfortable, unoccupied seating area in the lounge and sat down to wait. In just a few minutes, Dr. Blair Reed joined him. She was stunning, dressed in an expensive green suit that set off her beautiful red hair. He had forgotten how attractive she was. Blair Reed was five-foot ten, probably about one hundred twenty pounds, and could be easily described as a classic beauty. As he stood, she kissed him on the cheek. Then she took a seat next to him, rather than across from him.

Based on the way she had acted during their recent telephone call, he was not sure how to start the conversation, so he just told her, "It's good to see you again." She responded with the same statement.

When the cocktail waitress appeared, they ordered their drinks. Bob then asked, "Tell me, why you are here?" She realized Bob did not care what kind of business meeting she was attending. What he really wanted to know was why this meeting instead of telling him on the telephone about Shirley.

"Since I know you and Shirley were involved, I thought it best to tell you in person what has happened to her. When she moved back home to care for her parents, she started dating an old flame she had known from her college days. Shortly after they started seeing each other, she discovered she was pregnant. A couple of weeks later, they were married." Bob appeared to be stunned by the news. Blair added, "By the way, she said to tell you she did not think you are the father." After a few seconds when it was obvious Bob was contemplating that news, Blair broke the silence and asked, "So how is it going for you here in San Francisco?"

Bob related what he could about his work but talked mainly about the long hours he worked and the lack of social interaction. Almost all the agents in the office are married. Occasionally he would be invited to one of their homes for dinner. The only females he had contact with were at work, and most of them were married too. He was married to his work. After a couple of drinks, Bob asked, "What are you doing for dinner this evening?"

She did not have any commitments, so he suggested he take her out to dinner in his world, Chinatown. Blair gave him a thumbs up and off they went to the Hong Kong Clay Pot on Grant Avenue. Blair was a little surprised, given his language background, Bob seemed to stumble through the menu. He would explain to her later the reason he did not appear to understand or speak Mandarin in the restaurant. The food was great, and they spent a little time talking about Blair's work.

She apparently was "on the in" at Google but under a lot of stress. She too was married to her work. After dinner, he took her back to the hotel for a nightcap.

He asked, "What's your schedule for the remainder of the weekend?"

She said she was busy with meetings through Saturday evening and would be going back to San Jose on Sunday. He asked her if she would consider having lunch with him on Sunday before heading home. She said she would like that. Since she had her car at the hotel, she would come to Bob's apartment about 11 o'clock. He gave her the address on a cocktail napkin. This time, the goodnight kiss was on the lips, but not the passionate kind.

The next day, Blair arrived on time. He invited her in while he finished getting ready. He asked Blair how familiar she was with San Francisco. She had been there a number of times just for the day but had never spent any time in the city. He decided to take her on a drive to the Presidio for lunch, with the view of the Golden Gate Bridge and Baker Beach. It was a clear, crisp, winter day in San Francisco, so the viewing would be spectacular. Lunch at the Sessions at the Presidio was excellent. Blair wanted to know all about Bob and where he was from. He felt comfortable being truthful with her, but he knew he could not. Instead, he gave her the life history the Bureau made up for Robert Charles Allen.

He then asked Blair more about herself than he was able to glean from the previous evening. She was a computer science major in undergraduate school, received a master's degree in corporate management, and then went on to get a Doctor of Education. She planned on getting married, raising a family, and having a teaching career, but instead was recruited by Google. In the years she had been there, she had always had something to do with education and training, but recently has been tasked with working on broader issues. She is currently working with one of the attorneys in the general counsel's office on the development of new concepts and programs to be used by the industry to increase their marketing prowess. It involved discussions with other Big Tech companies, like Amazon, Facebook, YouTube, and Apple, because of regulatory rules and possible anti-trust issues. That's why she was in San Francisco. She found it interesting and enjoyed the work, but not some of the people she had to deal with.

The Big Tech people who worked at that level in their companies all seemed to live in "the fast lane." She frequently felt like she was looked at as the "sex object" from Google and not a real contributor. She did not like being put in that position. She admitted, "I may not be pure as the driven snow, but I don't sleep around, and I don't date married men." Bob understood. Blair was an incredibly beautiful woman, the kind most men are attracted to.

He was not sure what to say to her at that moment to keep from sounding sexist, so he punted. He suggested, "On that note I think we better get you headed back to San Jose." They drove back to Bob's apartment, Blair freshened up for the trip home, and Bob sent her on her way with, "I'll call you. OK?"

She smiled and said, "Please do." Bob was not quite sure where his relationship with Blair would be going. She was Shirley's friend, and she knew everything about his relationship with Shirley. Also, she could tell Bob still carried a torch for Shirley, even though she had moved on in life.

Over the next few weeks, Bob called Blair several times just to stay in touch. She seemed comfortable talking to him. She liked to talk about what she was doing at work and about some of the people she had to deal with. Bob was a good listener. He finally told her if she ever had reason to be in the city again, he would like to see her. She responded she would like that too. Then she added, "I need to get away some weekends and would love to come up to San Francisco to see more of the city."

It was a busy year for the Red Dragon Squad and Special Agent Bob Allen. The president's trade team was involved in trade negotiations with the Chinese. Most of the information about the Chinese comes from intelligence gathered overseas by the Central Intelligence Agency (CIA), but there is considerable intelligence gathered by FBI agents from sources here in the US. The sources developed by Bob and other agents on his squad provided information that the Chinese were not serious about negotiating permanent trade agreements

Out of the blue one evening, Bob got a call from Margaret Cassidy. She asked if Bob was still in San Francisco. She told him she was working at the Defense Intelligence Agency (DIA), in Washington, DC. She was going to be on the West Coast in the near future and expected to be overnight in San Francisco at least one evening. She wanted to know if they could meet for a drink. Bob did not see why not. He had no actual commitment to Blair or anyone else, and Margaret was a former classmate. Margaret said she would give him a call when her plans were confirmed.

A month or so later he got another call from Margaret Cassidy. She said her trip was on. She gave Bob her schedule, and it looked like she was going to be in San Francisco on a Friday night. He thought to himself, *She probably intentionally planned it that way, but that makes no difference.* Her plan was to stay at the Marine Memorial Club on Lower Nob Hill. She would fly into SFO midafternoon. Bob thought to himself, *It looks like drinks and dinner.*

When Margaret arrived, she took a cab from the airport to the hotel. She checked in, got out of her uniform, and freshened up. Then she slipped into a very sexy dress. When Bob got to the hotel, he called her on the house phone. A few minutes later, she presented herself in the lounge. She looked very good for a thirty-something woman. A big hug and a kiss between old friends was in order. Bob immediately noticed she was not wearing the wedding ring she wore when they were in Monterey.

The Marine Memorial Club was somewhat "old time," but it has a nice lounge area. Bob suggested they have a drink there and talk about where to go to dinner. Margaret thought that would be a good idea. When their drinks came, she started asking Bob about what he had been up to. Leaving out his relationships with Shirley and Blair, he gave her an unclassified review of his time in San Francisco. She asked about whether he got to use his Mandarin language training very much. He told her most of the people he was involved with spoke English, so he did not use it with them. Occasionally, he had to deal with someone who did not speak English, so with them he speaks Chinese. She related she did not get to converse in Mandarin often either. Most of her work was reviewing and analyzing translated material and rarely looking at original Chinese documents.

Bob asked her about her marital situation. She told him originally the Navy planned to send her to Japan so she would be co-billeted with her husband. When they found out he was planning to divorce her, Navy Personnel Command (NAVPERS) offered her a couple of alternative assignments: Pacific Command in Hawaii or the DIA. Knowing that Hawaii was an expensive place to live, she decided a divorcee would be better off in Washington, DC. Besides, she had already had one assignment in Hawaii. The other piece of good news was she had been selected for promotion to Commander (O-5). The latter news called for another drink. Bob suggested they have it with dinner. Given Margaret's good news, he suggested Northern Italian at the Acquerello Restaurant. It was first class. It had been a long day, so after dinner Bob took her back to the hotel. He offered to drive her to the airport in the morning. She indicated she would appreciate it.

Margaret's flight was to San Diego. She was ready to go when Bob arrived at the hotel. Saturday morning is not a particular busy time for traffic in the city, so the trip to the airport did not take long. During the ride, Margaret mentioned she really enjoyed the previous evening and hoped they would see each other again. She suggested if Bob ever had occasion to be in the Washington, DC, area, she hoped he would give her a call. Bob said he would. When they arrived at the departure gate, Bob unloaded her luggage, and she said good-bye to him like she was going to be gone for a long time. He did not flinch and enjoyed the moment. She turned and disappeared into the terminal. Bob was disoriented for just a moment but quickly got his bearings. He jumped into his car, deciding to go by the office before taking the rest of Saturday off.

In the summer of 2018, things picked up considerably when the president went to Singapore for a summit with Kim Jong-Un, the leader of North Korea. Bob had several Chinese informants who reported on the thinking of the

Chinese. Intelligence suggested there was much concern in the Chinese government about the president's trip lessening the Chinese influence over Kim.

Bob called Blair periodically, seemingly just to check on her, but knowing full well he was hoping to see her sooner rather than later. She seemed to always have something at work, which required her attention. Then one long weekend, she said she had a few days off and wanted to come up to San Francisco. Bob told her to come on up, and she could have his bedroom. He would sleep on the couch.

She replied, "Bob, don't be silly. That won't be necessary." The weekend was set. Now all Bob had to do was to make sure nothing happened at the office.

It was a magnificent weekend. Bob was with the most beautiful woman in San Francisco. She was an excellent cook and prepared him a couple of wonderful meals. Bob began to start thinking about what it would be like to be married to someone like Blair. However, he also started thinking again about who she would be marrying: Robert Allen or Douglas Gregory? The weekend went too fast, and Bob spent too much time pondering the issue about his identity. On Sunday, when the weekend was over, they said good-bye and promised not to wait long to see each other again.

In February, the Chinese Year of the Dog changed to the Year of the Pig, a year of good fortune and wealth. Bob was single and living the good life. While as a government employee, he was able to get by without going into too much debt, he was looking forward to a promotion. He also started thinking again about his future and putting money aside. At almost twenty-seven years of age, he was an eligible bachelor and probably considered an exceptionally good catch. That is, until someone looked at his personal finances. You do not live in San Francisco on the cheap.

It was another busy year for the Red Dragons and the analysts working counter-intelligence matters in the San Francisco Office. In June 2019, the president of the United States went to Korea for talks with South Korean President Moon Jae-in and a visit to the Korean Demilitarized Zone. These visits really light up the intelligence sources, especially when the president was invited by Kim to step across the demarcation line and into the Democratic People's Republic of North Korea (DPRK). The Chinese knew they could rein in the DPRK any time they wanted but were worried the US might extract even moderate concessions from Kim. However, the agreement by the DPKR to discontinue long-range missile tests was acceptable to Beijing. China did not want the North Koreans having missiles they could use to start a war which would then involve them.

Meanwhile, Bob continued in contact with Chen. He usually had some information to report. The meeting was always surreptitious. This time, their

October meeting was not about the information he had overheard from the old men at the store. Chen related he had some Chinese friends who were baggage handlers at the San Francisco International Airport. He learned from one of his friends that a few days earlier, there was a suspicious package smuggled in on a China Eastern/United Airlines direct flight from Wuhan. The reason the baggage handler was suspicious is on the airplane's arrival from China, when they unloaded the hold of the airplane, they were told not to unload one particular package. It was left in the hold. The unloaded passenger luggage and packages were taken to the US Customs area. The airplane was then towed to a parking area for cleaning until its scheduled return to China the next day. The cleaning person, who sweeps out the hold, removed the package and put it in a bag he had in his vehicle. The rest of the baggage handlers did not say anything because they were told it was a high priority medical shipment. It was supposedly some kind of vaccine, and if sent through US Customs, it would have to be opened and might spoil.

Chen's baggage handler friend did not know what happened to the package after it was removed from the airplane. All he could tell Chen was the package was a medium-sized box, and it was cold, like something packed in dry ice. It had a name on it, but no passenger luggage tag. The baggage handler did not see the name on the box. There was no medical or hazardous material symbols on it.

Bob thanked Chen for the information but did not know what to make of it. Back in the office, Bob got with Ted Lu and tried to figure out what they had. The method used to smuggle in the package was a little unusual. The fact the box was cold meant the contents were probably perishable. That eliminated the probability of an ordinary drug shipment. It must have been something important enough to risk putting in the hold of an airplane where it could have been found by anyone. Normally, information about a smuggling operation would just be passed to US Customs for handling, but this one seemed to be different. Bob took it to the ASAC who agreed they should send it to the Bureau as information from an SI. The secured message was sent electronically.

➤➤ Chapter 6 ◀◀

Xi Jinping is a politician who came to power in China in 2012 as the general secretary of the Communist Party (CCP) and as chairman of the Central Military Commission. In 2013 he cemented his control in China when he became the president of the People's Republic of China. He is known for the centralization of authority under his personal control; the implementation of rules and regulations that control the flow of ideas, culture, and capital out of the country; and the projection of power. He was responsible for a concept called the "Chinese Dream."

The Chinese Dream is basically the plan for China to replace the United States as the leading military and economic power in the world. The Chinese think in terms of millennia and not just in years. It does not have to be done now. It just has to be done eventually. Xi felt it was his job to put and keep his country on this course. As have been most of the Chinese leaders over the past hundred years, Xi is very authoritarian. If misleading the world as to his intentions is required, so be it. Whatever it takes to advance the Dream and his agenda.

When Donald J. Trump was elected as the forty-fifth president of the United States in November 2016, Xi knew immediately the Chinese would have to change the way they dealt with the US. For years, the Chinese had taken advantage of America by pirating its businesses in exchange for cheaper or less expensive products. He knew Trump would immediately engage China in trade negotiations designed to reduce America's trade deficit and to compel American businesses to divest themselves in China. Not to be deterred, Xi knew he would have to appear to act one way but at the same time continue his quest.

The Chinese had a lot of notice that trade was going to be big issue if Trump were elected. In a campaign speech on June 28, 2016, Trump laid down a marker by announcing a plan to counteract unfair trade practices through tariffs. After he was elected and became the president, Trump called for targeted tariff enforcement in anti-subsidy and anti-dumping cases, and for a review of the US trade deficits. This triggered the Chinese leader to begin his charade. It began with a summit at Trump's Florida property, Mir-a-Lago, in April. The two-day summit concluded with a 100-day agreement to hold trade talks. This would be the beginning of a long-drawn-out stalling tactic by the Chinese to keep the US thinking they were reaching trade agreements, which would forever change the trade relationship between the countries.

The president had chosen a Washington, DC, lawyer as the US Trade Representative. Together with a former investment banker, then serving as the secretary of the Treasury, the two were appointed to handle all of the trade negotiations with China. The Chinese trade negotiator was Vice Premier Liu He.

By July 2017, the trade talks seemed to have failed. In January of the following year, Trump imposed tariffs on two of the major manufactured goods important to the Chinese export trade: washing machines and solar panels. Then in March, the US imposed more tariffs. His action apparently prompted some additional negotiations, and both countries lifted some tariffs in August. By December, there was an agreement for a ninety-day moratorium on additional tariffs, but not until May 1, 2019, was there any real agreement. Two days later, the Chinese reneged on the agreement they had just signed. As a consequence, Trump immediately banned Huawei, the company leading China and much of Europe in the 5-G race, from being able to buy anything from American companies.

In June 2019, at the G-20 Summit in Osaka, Japan, Trump agreed to no more tariffs if Xi agreed to buying more agricultural products from the US. By August, the Chinese had once again slowed their purchase of farm products. They were also manipulating the value of their currency. Once again, Trump imposed more tariffs. It was not until October 2019 when the Chinese finally agreed to a Phase 1 agreement on trade.

The trade negotiations had kept the United States at bay for most of the Trump administration's time in office. There was an election coming up in another year, which could give China relief from any agreements with Trump. Besides China had other tricks up their sleeve to keep the US from interfering with the China Dream.

Trade with the US was not the only issue China faced for world dominance. Projecting its military power was also necessary. Ever since the Japanese were defeated in WWII, the United States had been the dominant military power in Southeast Asia. The US controlled all the sea lanes, including the 110-mile-wide Formosa Strait between China and the Island of Taiwan, which China claimed. The US always kept a large naval presence in the South China Sea, which the Chinese objected to. This was the United States' way of denying control of the seas by China.

Xi knew not to provoke a war with the US, but he would continue building his military. He had no compunction about inclemently confronting both his neighboring nations and the US. For him, it was for the good of the cause. Since the takeover of Hong Kong in 1997, the Chinese have worked to consolidate their influence and control of areas lost during WWII or near the mainland. Taiwan is still on their list of countries to take over.

In recent years, the Chinese have projected their military power in the South China Sea by building up their military facilities in the Paracel and Spratly

Island chains, and by creating new artificial islands to support their claim for control. This area controls most of the world's shipping operations. The US regularly carries on Freedom of Operations missions in this area to challenge the Chinese claims.

While Xi would visit the United States and wear one face, back in China, he planned ways to disrupt what appeared to be conciliation with the US. Whether Trump was reelected for four more years or a new president was elected in 2020, it made no difference. Time is one the side of the Chinese. Until then, the Chinese would continue to game the system.

The next big projection of Chinese power would come in October 2019 when the Chinese government implemented a plan to test the ability of their adversaries to respond to a viral pandemic. Using viral technology acquired from the USAMRIID at Fort Detrick, the Chinese scientists had, through gain of function research, developed a coronavirus called SARS-CoV-2. Knowing it could be deadly to their own workers and population, they also worked on developing anti-virus treatments.

In the years before the Trump administration, China had become the pharmaceutical capital of the world. All the international prescription drug-producing companies had established a major presence in China. Among them was Pfizer, Inc.

It did not take much planning for the Chinese government to introduce the virus into the Wuhan open-air wet market. The use of the market to spread the virus provided deniability. There was going to be some loss of life in Wuhan, but those working on the project were given the virus vaccine developed by the Chinese in advance of the release. Spread of the virus in China was also reduced by the immediate implementation of a domestic travel ban outside of Wuhan. However, international travel from the airport in Wuhan to San Francisco, Canada, Italy, and several other countries was not prohibited. This allowed the virus to spread outside of China.

In late November 2019, the FBI in San Francisco began receiving reports of a virus outbreak in the city of Wuhan. Shortly thereafter, Zhang Zhan, a thirty-seven-year-old Chinese lawyer turned journalist, started reporting a coronavirus epidemic in Wuhan. Beijing denied the story, and attempts were made by the Chinese government to cover up the viral outbreak in Wuhan. Arrests were made to put a damper on the story. At the same time, the government's severe restrictions on the movement of people from Wuhan to other parts of China kept the virus from developing in Beijing and the other major cities of China. As the word about the virus spread, the Chinese government then began to make false statements about the outbreak, claiming the virus originated from bats being sold in the wet market of Wuhan. While the story kept evolving, the Chinese government claimed not to be involved or concerned.

Eventually the virus which caused the epidemic was identified as SARS-CoV-2, a gain-of-function coronavirus developed in a laboratory. It did not come from bats. When that happened, the Wuhan Institute of Virology laboratory immediately became suspect. The lab is only a short distance away from the wet market area. The Chinese continued to deny the laboratory's involvement, and the story changed yet again. This time the Chinese claimed the virus was brought to Wuhan by US Army soldiers who were there for some military games. As the virus began to spread around the world, the World Health Organization (WHO) named the disease caused by the virus "COVID-19."

The first case of an illness from exposure to the SARS-CoV-2 virus was reported in December to a Chinese wet market employee. Within days the Chinese government reported to the World Health Organization (WHO), there were twenty-seven additional deaths in Wuhan from the virus. None of the information was made public until three weeks after the first case. Even then, the Chinese denied there was a problem. When it became evident there was, in fact, an epidemic in Wuhan, the WHO played down the problem by announcing there was no evidence of human-to-human transmission of the virus. Within days, a case of COVID-19 was reported in Thailand. Two days later, the first case was reported in the United States. The US victim was a traveler from Wuhan. Cases began popping up in Europe and then other countries. A pandemic was on, except in China. Eventually cases did appear in Hong Kong that were probably reintroduced into Hong Kong by an infected traveler from outside the country.

With the US and the world involved in a pandemic, little attention would be paid to what China was doing to move forward on the China Dream. The American media was not interested in who or what the cause was for the pandemic. The Trump administration was fully engaged in trying to stem the spread of the virus. At the same time, the US was working to develop a vaccine for it. Using a program designated as "Project Warp Speed" the government partnered with pharmaceutical companies to develop and produce an effective vaccine. The first company in the US to develop and commercially produce an effective vaccine was none other than Pfizer, Inc.

While the Trump administration was still engaged with trying to overcome the Russia–Russia Scandal, the trade negotiations with China stalled. While the US was attempting to keep the Chinese military in check and at the same time trying to control the viral pandemic unleashed by the Chinese, the Chinese intelligence apparatus was engaged in programs to sabotage President Trump's 2020 reelection. The Chinese were exercising control of the narrative about COVID-19 and everything else they were involved in. When you have control of the narrative, you have power.

→→ Chapter 7 ←←

I t was turning out to be a good year for Bob Allen's relationship with Blair Reed. She was able to get away from her work with Google at least one weekend a month and would spend her free weekends with Bob in San Francisco. In March, he had been in San Francisco two years. He knew his way around the city and Northern California. The trips to the Wine Country in Napa Valley were especially enjoyable. Blair got Bob to switch from being a beer drinker to being a wine devotee. Most of all, they just enjoyed being together and talking. One weekend, she even told him that Shirley had twin boys. Shirley and her husband named one of the boys Robert and the other Charles. Ouch! Bob questioned himself, *Why would she do that?* This revelation would play on Bob's conscience.

Blair also liked to discuss her problems at work with him since Bob was a good listener. While Blair's position at Google provided her a very good salary and a first-class lifestyle, she worried about the propriety of some of the projects she worked on and some of the people she came in to contact with. The lawyer she had recently been working with came from a large Washington, DC, law firm, and always seemed to be

71

willing skirt around what she considered was ethical. The people from other Big Tech firms they dealt with were sometimes of the same ilk. Too often, she was not comfortable with what they seemed to be trying to do, but it was not her call. The business of the Big Tech companies should be collecting data and making it available to those who need or can use it for their own purposes. Instead, Big Tech seemed to spend a lot of time and effort on colluding to limit new competition or choose what information would be made available to some and not to others. Censorship of information seemed too prevalent. The use of the Section 230 of the Communications Decency Act of 1996 exemption was a primary example. It was like the Big Tech companies were using their power to take control of the industry, the market, the economy, and the future of the country.

As a result of his continuing conversations with Blair, Bob began to wonder if the Chinese government was involved with any of the policy decisions being made by Big Tech. The six biggest tech firms, Amazon, Facebook, Twitter, Google, Microsoft, and Apple were all American companies, and all had interests in China. Certainly, they were subject to Chinese influence. Pressure by the Chinese government could lead to all kinds of problems for the US. Bob thought he might ask his sources to be on the lookout for any information about this. One must be careful about asking intel sources to report specific information. A double agent might intentionally feed misinformation back to you.

Even a source who is not playing both sides sometimes makes up information just to have something to endear them to the handler.

Occasionally, when Blair had a business weekend social function in the Silicon Valley, she would invite Bob to join her, if he was available. Everyone knew Dr. Reed was not married. She would just introduce Bob by name. Everyone probably assumed he worked for Google. No mention was ever made of his being an FBI agent, and no one seemed to remember him from the ski trip weekend at Lake Tahoe or seeing him at any parties with Shirley.

Most of the people who work for Big Tec companies are kind of leftist leaning. Because Blair had to deal with these people on an everyday basis, she did not feel comfortable having them associate her with someone who was from the FBI. Bob understood her concerns, and when asked, he just passed himself off as an entrepreneur. Fortunately, he was always able to by-pass security, if there was any.

The people Bob met at these functions were generally high- and mid-level executives. The presidents and CEOs would occasionally make an appearance, usually just to give a speech to the gathering. Interesting enough the "chiefs" were rarely ever seen together, even when they were at the same event. If they were meeting, it must have been during private dinners. Blair explained that when any of the chiefs needed to coordinate anything with anyone, whether one of the Big Tech companies, the government, or someone else, other executives were tasked to do it. The chiefs tried to stay above any fray. Typical of this is the work she was doing with the attorney from the general counsel's office.

As Bob began attending more of these get-togethers with Blair, he began to get to know some of the second- and third-level executives. He remembered how she described them during one of her earlier weekends with him. He agreed with her description and avoided talking to them about much of anything, except the San Francisco Giants baseball team and the San Francisco 49ers. As he was trained, Bob was a listener. He began to understand more about the industry. It set him to wondering about such things as anti-trust laws and Communications Act violations these companies were engaged in. These issues were outside of his area of responsibility in the San Francisco office, but he thought he should discuss them with his supervisor, ASAC Furginson. Whatever he did, Bob wanted to keep Blair out of it. She was a girlfriend, not a source.

Back in the office, Bob discussed with ASAC Furginson what he had picked up in his social contacts with people from Big Tech. Bob laid out the whole situation, what Blair had told him, and what he had learned over the course of going to business functions with her. Furginson was impressed with non-Chinese contacts Bob had made in a little over two years in San Francisco.

After discussing what Bob had learned from Blair, plus his own observations, the conclusion was there was not enough information of a criminal act for the FBI to open a case. That is the difference between the criminal side of the house and the counter-intelligence side in which Bob works. The supervisor, however, was glad to know Bob had an apparent in at Google and had met some of the players in Silicon Valley. It might come in useful if anything should develop.

Most of the intelligence information Bob collected from his sources, and from listening to discussions in Mandarin when he was in Chinatown, was about the trade talks and Chinese election interference. Little of it was what could be considered hard fact, but almost uniformly what he heard was that that Xi Jinping was not negotiating in good faith and was stalling until the 2020 presidential election.

Back in the office, Bob was preparing for the day's work when his cell phone rang. It was Woody calling to tell him there had been another inquiry about the friend from Hamilton. Bob still had not a clue why the Chinese were interested in Douglas Gregory. The Bureau was going to look at it to see if they could determine any particular reason for the interest at this time or if it was just a periodic check. They were trying to decide if it was time to "run the flag up the pole" and see what happens. If any decision was made, they would get back to him.

It did not take long. It was just a few days after Bob submitted the information about the smuggled shipment, Woody called again. They wanted him back in Washington, DC, for discussions and possibly a special assignment. Woody did not say why, only to bring some winter clothes and plan to be there at least a couple of weeks. Bob was not sure if this had to do with the smuggled package, the conference he had with the supervisor about Silicon Valley issues, or the inquiry about "his friend" from Hamilton.

Before flying back to Washington, DC, on Sunday, Bob and Blair spent the weekend together in San Francisco. He told her he was called back to the Bureau for something important and hoped he would not be gone long. He hinted that he also had a personal issue to resolve but did not say what. If he could get back for Christmas, he would.

➤➤ Chapter 8 ⟵⟵

Late Sunday, Bob took a red-eye flight to Dulles Internight Airport and was at the Bureau by 8 a.m. A few minutes later he was in Woody's office. Not knowing for sure why he was there, Bob simply asked, "What's happening?" Woody replied by asking him if he ready for a change in scenery, to which Bob answered, "No."

Woody then related the reason they brought Bob Allen (or Douglas Gregory) in was that the National Security Branch (NSB) people thought this might be a good time to see why the Chinese were so interested in Douglas Gregory. It also might be an opportunity to run a counter-intelligence operation. Bob was not sure what the Bureau had in mind, but he was glad to find out this was not about the information Blair had passed on to him about the activities in Silicon Valley. He did not want to get Blair involved in anything, except maybe his love life.

Moments later, NSB Supervisor Jack Lewis walked into Woody's office and introduced himself. Woody told Bob that Jack has been responsible for keeping up a fictious dossier on Gregory, and it appeared the Chinese periodically checked on him. They thought it was time to find out why.

Lewis then told Bob the story they created on Doug. Starting with his Air Force Reserve Commission from the Air National Guard, after graduation from law school, he entered Air Force flight training program. As a top graduate, he was selected to fly the new F-22 Raptor. Throughout the dossier, Gregory is portrayed as a "Fast Burner." By being in a highly classified flying program, they were able to keep moving him around so the Chinese could not verify where he really was at any given time. Credit card purchases were made in different places and financial information was added to his credit reports, leaving a trail which could be checked, but always too late to timely locate him. The FBI even created class graduation photos of him with flying school classmates, which are on the internet. The call sign name on his flying helmet was "Waldo."

It would have been hard for the Chinese intelligence services to pierce the veil of the cover story. The latest addition to the story is that Air Force Captain Douglas Gregory has been tapped for reassignment to a secret project in the Pentagon, dealing with the program development of a new fighter aircraft. The idea was to have Gregory show up in DC to see if the Chinese would try to contact him. It sounded to Bob like this was more than just a two-week special assignment.

Lewis told him, "The Bureau would not run it too long. If the Chinese did not try to contact Doug Gregory within a reasonable period of time, the Air Force would move him out of the "Puzzle Palace" and the Bureau would send Allen back to San Francisco or find another assignment for him. Bob was not enthusiastic with being gone from Blair and San Francisco, but he knew this had been a long-term project, and he agreed to it when he signed on as a special agent.

Lewis then asked if Bob was acquainted with anyone in the Washington, DC, area. He acknowledged knowing Margaret Cassidy. Lewis asked, "Who is she?" Bob related she was a divorced naval officer who had been a classmate in Mandarin language school in Monterey and now worked at the DIA. He had not been in touch with her for some time, but she did look him up when she was in San Francisco in April or May last year.

Lewis though about it for a moment, and then said, "Don't look her up until we have had a chance to run a check on her." Bob agreed.

In the meantime, Lewis suggested Bob stay at the Harrington for a couple of days and come into the office for some training on how to avoid detection by Chinese intelligence. If the Chinese decided to make contact, they would undoubtedly take photographs of him and run them through their photograph recognition system. While they probably did not have any suitable photographs of him from when he was in college or law school, they most certainly had photos of SA Bob Allen of the San Francisco FBI office. Lewis suggested Bob wear a hat and try to cover part of his face. A Bureau makeup artist would show him how to change his facial recognition just enough the Chinese may not be able to confirm Douglas Gregory and Robert Allen are one and the same.

Bob called Blair to tell her he was going to disappear for a few weeks but not to be concerned and not to call him. His personal cell phone would forward all his calls to his office in San Francisco, and they would not necessarily know how to contact him. He would try to get home as soon as he could and would try to call her if possible.

A couple of days later Bob was again in the office of Jack Lewis. He was told that for the duration of this assignment he was now Captain Douglas Gregory, USAF. He was issued an Air Force military identification card and Pentagon building passes, all in the name of Captain Douglas Gregory and a set of FBI credentials with his real name on them. Lewis also advised Margaret Cassidy was considered a good risk, and Doug could go ahead with contacting her. He could tell her the reason for his change of identity but not to discuss any details of the operation. She might serve as a good cover, but there was no sense putting her in jeopardy.

With his new cell phone, issued by the FBI, he called Margaret. She was surprised to receive a call from Bob on a telephone with a Northern Virginia area code and number. He told her it was a long story, and he was going to be in the area for a while. Before he could say anything else, she suggested they meet for a drink. Bob told her he was available and needed one. When she found out he was staying in the District (Washington, DC), she suggested he grab the Metro and take the Orange Line to the Virginia Square-GMU Station. She would pick him up there in an hour.

When Margaret recognized "Bob" leaving the station, she blew her horn and yelled out the window at him. He jumped in the front passenger seat of her car and tried to give her a big hug. She was a step ahead of him. She planted a big kiss on him.

Then she said, "Let's go get that drink." She drove to the Ritz Carlton in Pentagon City, and they found a quiet sofa in the lounge. She asked immediately, "So what brings you to Washington, DC, and why didn't you call me before you got here?"

Bob asked her how much time she had. She replied, "All night if necessary."

He told her, "I am here to meet somebody from the other side. It is all on the up and up. The FBI is using me as bait to identify what they think may be a Chinese spy-recruiting operation. You are the only person I can tell because you might be able to provide me some cover. For this operation, I am Captain Douglas Gregory, USAF, assigned to a highly classified program at the Pentagon. Forget the name Robert Allen. Just refer to me as Doug."

She asked, "Where are you going to live while you are here?"

He told her he did not yet know, but he could not stay in the hotel. He needed a permanent address not too far from the Pentagon.

Without hesitation she said, "I have an extra bedroom in my house. Why don't you rent it from me? My house is close to the Metro Orange Line, which has a station in the Pentagon."

Doug had mixed feeling about her offer. He was concerned about developing an intimate relationship with Margaret while he was seeing Blair. At the same time, it was the perfect living situation since Margaret was now part of his protection plan. He asked to think about it.

Margaret then asked, "Do you remember our classmate you use to refer to as Spooky 2? He is on assignment to a special task force at DIA. I get to see him all the time."

Doug told her not to mention anything to Spooky about seeing him or his being in town. Maybe when the sting operation was over, the three of them could get together.

After a couple glasses of wine, Margaret suggested they go back to her house so Doug could see the room she has available, and so she could fix them something to eat. Her home in Arlington was not too far from the Metro Station where she had picked him up. It was a three-bedroom house in a nice neighborhood. She headed straight to the kitchen and fixed a delicious dinner from the freezer. Her wine selection at home was good too. After a relaxing meal, she took him on a tour of her home. She had converted one of the bedrooms into a den with lots of naval memorabilia and some Chinese artwork. The guest bedroom was very comfortable and looked like it had been decorated for a man. Then she showed him her bedroom and invited him to try out the bed. She laughed when he just sat on the side of the bed and patted the mattress.

Doug acknowledged he had enjoyed the evening and seeing Margaret again. He had a lot to do the next day and told her he would call about renting the room. She drove him into the District and dropped him at the Harrington. It did not take long for him to crash. It had been a busy day.

The next morning, Doug called Jack Lewis to brief him on the offer he had to rent a room from Margaret. Since Doug was single, Lewis did not see problem. He reminded Doug not to get her involved in the operation. On Sunday, they would launch the sting. Doug called Margaret on the FBI cell phone and told her she had a tenant. She offered to pick him up in the District after work, but he told her just to pick him up at the Metro Station at 1700 hours. The response was, "Aye, Aye, Mate." Bob checked out of the Harrington and had them hold his luggage in the baggage room until later in the day. He walked around the shopping area near Wisconsin Avenue, NW. The only thing he bought was a disposable cell phone, for which he paid cash.

Then he took the Metro to the Pentagon station. At the top of the escalator, he scanned his building pass. He was in. This was his first time in the Pentagon. It would become a part of his daily morning routine. Anyone checking the entry logs of the Pentagon would assume he must be going to work there. He had lunch in the mall and then walked the halls to familiarize himself where the various agencies and offices were. In the late afternoon, he exited the building. No record was being made of the people leaving the Pentagon. He picked up his suitcases at the Harrington, then purchased a good bottle of Napa Valley Cab at a nearby wine store and got back on the Metro to meet Margaret.

When he got into Margaret's car, she greeted him with a "Good afternoon, Captain."

That brought a smile to his face. In the car, they were like a married couple. A kiss on the cheek. She drove home. Tonight was pizza night, ordered in.

She loved his choice of wine and said, "The wine opener is on the kitchen counter. Welcome aboard!" Then she disappeared. A few minutes later she came back in wearing an attractive casual outfit. He took off his coat and tie. She ordered the pizza, and he poured the wine. They adjourned to the living room and toasted each other.

She wanted to know more about what he had been up to. Margaret had met Shirley at one of the class Chinese community events in Monterey, but she did not know anything about Blair. He told her Shirley left

California and went home to care for her parents and married someone she knew from college. Other than that, there was not much he could talk about. He still had the apartment Margaret had helped him pick out and decorate. He said he worked 24/7 and was married to his job. He asked what she had been doing since they last saw each other.

She said she got her promotion to O-5 and now headed up a desk, evaluating intel received on the Chinese military, mostly their Navy. Some of the material she received was printed material written in Mandarin. If she had a hard time understanding something, she would get Spooky 2 to help her. She spent most of her time writing analysis reports. It was not very exciting. Doug asked about her love life. She told him she dates some but really was not interested in getting married again, at least not while she is still in the Navy. Maybe when she retires, she will meet someone who is "Mr. Right," and they can move to Florida. She indicated until then all she needed was a lover.

Doug needed another glass of wine. The pizza delivery was there, so Margaret answered the door. Sitting in the kitchen was a little less intimidating to Doug. It gave him a chance to change the subject. He said he did not know much about Margaret and asked for her to fill him in. She grew up in Maryland where her father was a professor at the University of Maryland. He worked a lot for the Army facility at Fort Detrick. Her mother was an elementary school teacher. She had no brothers or sisters. After high school, she attended the US Naval Academy, and it was there she met her future husband. He was in the class ahead of her. She was a military history major and after graduation, became an intelligence officer. Brad, her ex-husband, finished pilots training about the time of her graduation, and they were married in the chapel at Annapolis. The Navy had been good to her, co-billeting her with Brad, except when he had carrier duty. While she was in school in Monterey, he found a Geisha he liked better - end of story.

Now that they were fully acquainted, Doug told her the FBI plan was now in full swing, and he needed her to have dinner out with him on Sunday evening. She said it sounded exciting. She was not to be involved with the operation except as a cover for him, and he could not tell her what was happening or why. She was to just roll with the punches. As far as anyone they came into contact with, he was an Air Force officer who worked at the Pentagon and rented a room from her. They had no history.

Before going to bed, she warned him that she slept in the nude and had a bad habit of getting up in the middle of the night for a snack. She told him not to be embarrassed if he happened to be awake and saw her.

He laughed and said, "I am sure I would enjoy seeing such a beautiful women au naturelle."

On Saturday, Margaret drove him around the District, and then they went shopping in Northern

Virginia. He purchased another disposable cell phone for use in the operation. The following afternoon, he used the second cell phone to make a reservation for two at a Chinese restaurant near the State Department, where he might be able to make his first contact.

Shortly before leaving the house on Sunday, Doug used the cell phone he had purchased in the District to call a special number the FBI had given him. All he said was, "This is Waldo. Dinner is at seven."

Before going to dinner, Doug told her, "Leave your Mandarin at home. Just talk in English. Do not act like you recognize anything I or anyone else may say in Chinese. Listen and you can tell me later if you overhear anything interesting." She understood.

When they arrived at the restaurant they were seated by an elderly hostess. Doug greeted her and then thanked her in Mandarin. She did not say anything in return, but Doug noticed she went straight to one of the waiters. That waiter then came to the table and greeted Doug and Margaret in Mandarin. Doug responded in Mandarin. Margaret did not flinch. She played her role well. When the waiter returned to the table to take their order, Margaret ordered in English and Doug ordered in his best Mandarin. When the waiter brought the food, Doug suggested they speak in English so his lady friend could understand the conversation. The waiter agreed.

It was a fine meal, and both enjoyed it. When the waiter brought the dinner check, he commented on Doug's Chinese language ability and asked where he learned to speak it. Doug replied, "I took some courses in college." The waiter then asked if Doug had been in the restaurant before, to which Doug responded, "No. I am in the Air Force, and I have just arrived for an assignment at the Pentagon." The waiter then suggested if Doug would like to leave a business card, they would put him on a guest list for special events. Doug said, "I would like that," and handed the waiter his Air Force business card.

The card which Doug gave the waiter identified him as Captain Douglas Gregory, USAF, had a room number inside a secure area in the Pentagon which could not be reached directly from the hallways, and a telephone number that was answered by a recording. The FBI controlled this number on the Pentagon phone system. The first contact had probably been made. Now it was time to hurry up and wait.

⇢ Chapter 9 ⇠

On Monday morning, following dinner out at the Chinese restaurant, Margaret dropped Doug in the Pentagon parking lot on her way to work at the old Bolling AFB, where the DIA is located. Doug went through Pentagon security and headed toward the area in the Pentagon where the room on his card would be located. On the way he stopped in the men's room, washed his hands, and waited to see if he had a tail. Back in the hallway, he did not see anyone he had noticed before. Instead of entering the secure area, he headed to the mall in the Pentagon to have breakfast. After breakfast, he repeated the earlier routine of going to a restroom near the secure area. Again, he did not detect any surveillance of him. He headed for the Metro and took the Orange Line to the Federal Triangle Station. It was just a short walk to the J. Edgar Hoover Building.

His morning was another meeting with Jack Lewis. Doug thought the Sunday night dinner had gone well. Lewis said the report of the surveillance squad, who was there too, was positive. Their waiter was a known intelligence suspect. Now they would have to wait and see if anything developed.

Within a few days, there was another credit check on Douglas Gregory. It was beginning to look like the Chinese might have taken the bait. A few days later, there was a reported hack on the Pentagon's Photo Recognition System. It probably meant the Chinese were checking the identity of Captain Gregory. This was the weakest link in the identity chain. If the Chinese did not make a match with SA Robert Allen, the operation was probably in the clear. In the meantime, Doug followed his morning routine at the Pentagon, but not always going to the FBI building. Sometimes he just disappeared to someplace where there might not be photo identification cameras, which was not easy in Washington, DC. At the end of the day, he would make his way back to Virginia on the Orange Line, and Margaret would pick him up at the station.

Finally, about a week later, the telephone number on Doug's business card was called. A female voice said, "The is Jenney Ling from the Chinese restaurant where you dined recently, and we wanted to thank you for your business. We have selected you for a complimentary dinner with other customers who speak Mandarin. If you are interested, please give me a call at the restaurant."

Lewis called Doug on the FBI cell and said they needed to meet the following morning to discuss a possible contact. They concluded it might have been an attempt to set him up for a meeting or might be just a public relations call. In either event, Doug should respond to the call and see what happens. That evening,

Doug called the restaurant and asked for Jenny. He was told she was not on duty in the evenings, and if he left his name and telephone number, she would call him the next day. He left his name and the number of the disposable cellphone he purchased in Northern Virginia. Now it was time to just wait. Jenny called him back the next afternoon and invited him to dinner the following Monday night, if he was available. He indicated he was interested and appreciated the invitation. He then asked if he could bring a guest. He was told the dinner was for Mandarin speakers only. They already knew the lady who was with him before apparently did not speak the language. He accepted the invite. Doug called Lewis to report the next meeting was on for next Monday at the restaurant at 8 o'clock.

That gave Doug enough time to worry about the meeting. If it was an intelligence contact, they had not identified him as Robert Allen or the contact would not have been made. Margaret was out of the loop on what had been taking place since the Sunday night dinner and knew better than to ask. Margaret could tell Doug seemed to be under a lot of stress. She decided to make it a relaxing weekend for him if she could.

Doug had more on his mind than the sting operation. He had not talked to Blair since leaving California and was wondering about her. He did not want to talk to Blair while Margaret was present, so he told Margaret he had to go for a walk. So she did not worry about it being some surreptitious FBI meeting, he told Margaret he was just going to walk in the neighborhood to clear his head. He would be back within thirty or forty minutes.

When he was out of sight of the house, he called Blair on the DC disposable phone. He was afraid she would not answer since she would not recognize the number he was calling from, but she did answer. He was embarrassed for not having stayed in touch with her. Bob knew he could not tell her anything about what he had been doing in his absence from San Francisco. He apologized and said he just was not in a position to call her before now. She did not respond. He hoped the matter he was working on would be wrapped up in a few weeks and he could get back home. Finally, he said, "I miss you."

She was somewhat non-committal but did say she too hoped he would be home soon. He asked about her work, and all she would say is "It's crazy as hell." He told her not to call him on this telephone number unless it was an emergency. He would try to stay in touch with her more often. That was it. On the way back to Margaret's house, he began to worry Blair had, during his absence, probably decided to move on with her life. He felt she just might not want to say anything to him until he got back to San Francisco.

It was Saturday night, and Margaret had nothing planned except to take care of Doug. She prepared filet mignon on her grill and told Doug to find a bottle of wine from her collection. After dinner, she piled the dishes in the sink and told him to peel down to his shorts. She was going to give him a body massage. How could he resist an offer like that after such a fine meal? She changed into something more comfortable too. The wine had affected him, and he could not do anything but lay there and take it. She was an excellent masseuse. He had never felt so relaxed. Within minutes, he was in a torpor state. When he awoke, he was in her bed, and she was cuddled up next to him.

On Sunday, he told her he would be working late on Monday evening and not to pick him up at the Metro. If he had any trouble getting back to the house before the Metro stopped operating, he would call her. Not to worry; it was a meeting in a public place and the Bureau would have it covered. He was not in any jeopardy.

On Monday, after his daily trip to the Pentagon, he headed to the Bureau to see Jack Lewis. They went over the plan for the evening, and Doug was fitted with a bug. Doug went back to the Pentagon and killed time until the evening. From there, he took a taxi to the restaurant. If this was the real thing, they would ask the cab driver where his fare was picked up. The restaurant was open, but there were no customers around. Doug entered the restaurant and instead of the elderly hostess who met him before, he was met by the waiter they had earlier. Doug said he was here for the Mandarin speaker's dinner. It was then he realized the restaurant was closed to the public on Mondays. Knowing anything he said would be heard by nearby FBI audio people, he asked in English, "Are you closed tonight?" He got an affirmative answer, in English. He was then led to a private room where his host introduced herself as Jenny Ling.

Doug asked, "Is this it, or are we expecting others?" Jenny grinned a little and told him this was it. "A little unusual for a special restaurant dinner isn't it? Do I speak to you in English or Mandarin?" She told him English was fine.

Jenny asked him if he remembered Daniel Chen from his college days. Doug answered, "Of course, but I haven't seen or heard from him since then."

She related that she was a friend of Chen, that he was an important scientist in China, and he suggested she look Doug up and say hello for him.

He responded, "So this is more of a personal thing than a restaurant promotion?" She indicated it was. She proceeded to tell Doug that she had another job but sometimes helped at the restaurant with public relations. When Chen asked her to look Doug up, it was the best way she could think of to reach him. At that point, Doug knew it was an intelligence contact and not just social. There was no way Chen could know Doug had been in this restaurant a week earlier and had left his card with the private contact number.

Doug was in a situation where he would just have to play the game. He asked about his former acquaintance. Jenny had done her homework. She told him after Chen graduated from Ohio State, he got his master's degree from Johns Hopkins and then his doctorate at the University of Maryland. She then tried to make it personal by asking about Doug. He fed her some of the story the FBI had prepared for him. After dinner, she said she enjoyed meeting Doug and would send Chen a note. She also said she hoped to see Doug again, and he could always call the restaurant and leave a message for her. It was not an uneventful meeting.

After dinner, he decided to walk to the DuPont Circle Metro Station, in hopes the FBI "tech people" would meet him and take his wire. They did not, probably because he might be under surveillance by the other side. He called Margaret and told her he was getting on the Metro and would be at the station in Arlington in about twenty minutes.

The first thing he did when he got back to the house was to remove the wire and put it in his bedroom. It was probably still active, and he did not want anyone listening to his personal conversations with Margaret. She had a glass of wine waiting for him. She did not ask about his meeting. They talked a little about the news of the day before calling it a night.

On Tuesday morning, he made his usual trip to the Pentagon and followed the same routine he always did. Today he also had breakfast in the mall so he could do a double check to see if anyone was following him. He then went back to the secure area where he supposedly worked and made a restroom stop. No tail. Then he left the building and caught the Metro.

Doug and Lewis reviewed what happened the night before. Lewis had run Jenny Ling's name though the

Bureau's indices. Turns out she is a professional prostitute who works for a madame who runs a high-class brothel in a condominium apartment on Wisconsin Avenue, NW. The girls who work there cater to congressmen, judges, and other government officials. They agreed Jenny's meeting with Doug was probably a set-up for a honey trap operation.

This called for a Plan B. The Bureau was not going to throw away a special agent by letting him take the bait offered. Also, they did not want Doug to appear too anxious to see Jenny again. Lewis suggested if Doug wanted to take some time off, this might be a good time. Doug immediately thought of flying back to San Francisco to see Blair.

Lewis then instructed, "When you buy your ticket, you are to travel as Doug Gregory, and we don't want Bob Allen anywhere near the office in San Francisco. Stay away from the Chinese community while you are there too. We will call you if something develops; otherwise we will see you back here in a week."

Chapter 10

Before buying an airline ticket, he thought he better talk to Blair to make sure he was not persona non grata with her. It would not be much fun being in San Francisco without seeing her. Bob decided to call Blair at Google. He got her voicemail, but about a half hour later, she called him back. He told her he had some time off and was coming home for a few days. She seemed pleased. He told her he would probably be there by Friday and asked if she could come to San Francisco for the weekend. She said "yes," and asked him to just let her know his schedule. With that, Captain Doug Gregory went back to the Pentagon to purchase his ticket at the Sato Travel Office.

If the Chinese are still checking on him, it is likely they will know he will be flying to wherever he buys a ticket for. If so, they will likely be following him too. He does not need that. What he needs is to make sure they do not know he is in San Francisco. At the Pentagon, he bought a one-way ticket to Las Vegas.

He surprised Margaret that evening when he told her he was going back to California for a few days. Nothing has changed about what he was doing here, but things had gone quiet. He needed to take care of a few things back in San Francisco in case events here take longer than hoped. She suspected his personal business in San Francisco also included a relationship, although he had never talked about it.

The next morning, he went through his normal routine. When he left the Pentagon, instead of taking the Metro to the Federal Triangle, he took the bus to Dulles Airport. Before boarding the flight, he took a good look at the people who would be on the flight with him. If he was being followed, there was nothing he could do about it during the flight, so he just relaxed. When they landed at McCarran Field in Las Vegas, before going to the baggage claim area, he used his DC disposable phone to make a reservation on the next flight to San Francisco. He then claimed his suitcases and exited the terminal in the passenger pick-up area. He found a bench outside and sat down to wait like he was being picked up. He did notice a few people from his flight, but most of them disappeared before he left the area. Then shortly before the time for his flight to San Francisco, he went to the ticket counter and checked in. At the boarding gate, he took another look around to see if he recognized anyone. He did not see a tail, if there was one. Just to make sure, when they started boarding the flight, he continued to sit in the gate area until they made the final boarding call. Doug was the last person to board. He figured if someone was following him, they would not have boarded before he did, in case he decided not to board at all. The flight to San Francisco was an hour and thirty-five minutes.

From the airport in San Francisco, he took the Bay Area Rapid Transit (BART) and then a taxi to his apartment complex. He had the driver drop him in a different part of the apartment complex. When he entered his apartment, it smelled stale, but he was glad to be home. If he had a tail he was sure one had been able to stay with him on the trip.

The next morning, he put the battery back in the car to see if it would start. Bingo! He went to the grocery store and spent some time talking to his neighbors. They wanted to know where Bob had been. He waived them off by just saying he was working out of town. He spent the afternoon cleaning the apartment and then went for a drive to the Presidio. He was sure no one had found Douglas Gregory in San Francisco. In the evening, he called Blair and told her he was home. She said she had taken the afternoon off on Friday and would drive up then. He liked that and said, "It sounds like a plan."

On Friday morning, he found a local florist and bought her some red roses. He went to the wine store and purchased a couple of bottles of good wine. He ate lunch out so he would not mess up his kitchen. He ordered a gourmet meal of veal marsala delivered at supper time; all was in readiness for Blair's arrival. He just hoped she was not going to tell him she was breaking it off. He had not had any real indication from her about her feelings toward him since he had been away.

Blair arrived about 5 o'clock. He saw her get out of the car, so he went out to meet her. It was an affectionate meeting, which made him feel more comfortable. Once she freshened up, Bob popped the cork on an excellent bottle of Pinot Grigio from Italy. He could not take his eyes off her. He was sure she was the most beautiful redhead in San Francisco. He told her they were eating in tonight and would explain why later. He almost forgot to give her the red roses, which had already put in a vase for her. Dinner arrived on time. Blair said she was impressed by how much he had done to prepare for her visit. After dinner, Bob opened a bottle of Cabernet from Napa Valley. He then said, "I need to talk to you."

She interrupted him and said, "I have something important to tell you too, and maybe I should go first." He had an immediate sinking spell and thought, *Here it comes*. There was a moment of silence that seemed like an eternity. Then she said, "I am about to become the mother of twins."

It was not what he was expecting, and he was momentarily confused. She must have recognized it from the look on his face. She then went on to tell him that Shirley and her husband had been killed in an auto crash. The boys were not with them. Blair was their godmother and had agreed to raise them if anything ever happened to Shirley and her husband. The boys were with relatives until some legal issues in Texas were worked out, but she was preparing to adjust her life so she could take care of them. Bob was stunned, not so much about Blair becoming the mother of twin boys, but about Shirley's death.

He quickly recovered and said, "Well, I was about to complicate your life even more. Tomorrow I was going to propose to you. I still have a lot I don't know about you, but I have been in love with you for a long time, and I know you would make me happy. The only problem I have is you really don't know who I am. I don't want you to marry me and for you to be surprised by anything. I guess I need to tell you a few things before I even ask you."

She suggested he might want to wait a while about making a proposal to her. At least until after they talked and when both were not half inebriated. Blair said, "Pour me another glass of wine, and I will start."

Blair proceeded to tell Bob her family was from Georgia. Her paternal grandfather was a successful Atlanta lawyer who made a lot of money. Her father was somewhat of a ne'er-do-well golfer, who lived off family trusts set up by her grandfather. Her mother was an educator. Blair grew up in Sarasota, Florida. Her mother and father are both deceased. She has no siblings. Her mother encouraged her to work hard and succeed. She did her undergraduate work at the University of Florida, where she played on the Lady Gators Golf Team. She still plays and has a three handicap. She took her master's degree at Emory University in Atlanta and received her doctorate from Nova Southeastern University. She has cousins, but none who are close. She added, "You already know what my life goals were. That's it! Any questions?"

That sounded like a serious response to the question of "Who am I?" To add a little levity to the conversation he asked, "What was you nickname in high school?' That brought a laugh from her.

She then said, "Your turn."

Bob proceeded carefully saying, "What I am about to tell you must be kept an absolute secret between you and me. I can't tell you everything at this time, but I am not who you think I am. Robert C. Allen is an alias given to me by the FBI. I cannot tell you at his time why or what my real name is. I hope when I finish my work in Washington, DC, I will be able to drop my cover name and get my life back. Then I will be able to tell you all about me before I became Bob Allen. Until then, I have to hope you will accept me as I am. Back at the Bureau, they refer to me as "your friend" when they were talking about my real identity."

She then wanted to know if she could ask questions. He told her to ask and he would answer, if he could. She asked, "Have you ever been married?" Without hesitation, he told her he had not. It was her only question.

The next morning, they slept in, which was a little unusual for both. After a brunch at home, Bob took her for a drive. He explained while he was home for a couple of days, he was not to go to the office or be out in public too much, for fear his cover in San Francisco and his assignment in Washington, DC, would be blown.

He headed up toward the Presidio and parked at Baker Beach. They had been there before.

Once there, he said, "Miss Reed, will you marry my friend?" That got a good laugh and a big smile from her.

Blair responded, "I guess you are telling me that Robert Allen is not proposing to me for himself but wants me to marry his friend at some future time?" That drew a smile from him too. He acknowledged she had it right. She then added, "Tell your friend, when he is able to speak for himself, I might be inclined to accept, unless there is something disappointing you haven't told me about him."

Bob was ready to move on. He wanted to get Robert Allen out of his life, but he was not in control of when or how to make it happen. By agreeing to go undercover some three years earlier, he had become indentured. He liked the work he was doing, but he did not like being SA Bob Allen anymore. He wanted to be Special Agent Douglas Gregory. He knew he had to get back to Washington, DC, again to make this happen.

Bob and Blair enjoyed the weekend together, even though they were mostly homebound. Blair went back to San Jose early Monday morning.

Captain Gregory called Jack Lewis. Doug said, "I am done here in SF for now and ready to get back to work. Are you ready for me?"

Lewis indicated they were, so Doug took a direct flight that afternoon to Dulles. Before leaving the airport in San Francisco, he called Margaret and told her he would be back late that evening but not to wait up. Then he called Blair to tell her he was going back to DC so he could work on unwinding the relationship between Bob Allen and his friend.

Chapter 11

Doug got back to Margaret's house rather late. He let himself in and heard Margaret in the kitchen. When he walked into the kitchen, there was Margaret sitting at the table in her bedroom attire, stark naked. He had been forewarned. He did not flinch and just sat down across the table from her like nothing was wrong.

When they were finished talking, Margaret detected he was not interested in sleeping with her that night, so she asked, "How was she?" She knew Doug had just been with someone else. Doug promised to tell Margaret about his trip to SF.

The next day she dropped him at the Pentagon, and he went through his regular routine. Hard telling if the Chinese had even picked up on his return. Doug was glad to see Jack Lewis again and wanted to know if there had been any developments. Lewis said they had not had any indication the Chinese were inquiring about him or his whereabouts while he was gone, and Jenny Ling had not called him. Lewis said, "It looks like they are waiting for you to call Jenny."

Lewis told Doug, "The people in the National Security Branch had relooked at the operation and decided to change gears. The Chinese plan to compromise you could go on a long time before they decide to change their modus operandi. Eventually the Chinese may try to introduce you to a recruiter, who may even be someone from the Chinese Embassy. In that case, the best we could hope for is likely to catch a second secretary or someone already known to us as a spy. Instead, the NSB had decided to try to double Jenny Ling. If we can do that maybe we will have another source we can use." That sounded like music to Doug's ears. Lewis laid out the plan they had devised. Doug asked Lewis if they could wait a day to implement the plan because he had already made some plans for this evening. Tonight he was having dinner with his landlord.

After killing time in the Pentagon, Greg decided to go home early. He picked up flowers in the mall floral shop and headed back to Virginia. On the way to Margaret's, he stopped at the grocery store and picked up something for dinner. He called her and left a message not to pick him up at the Metro. Then he went to work in her kitchen to prepare dinner. Tonight, they were having chicken cordon bleu and some green peas, both from the freezer section of the grocery store. He found a candle and set the table. He was not sure why he was doing this, except he knew they would be talking about his relationship with Blair, and he wanted Margaret to know he appreciated her too.

Margaret loved having dinner prepared by Greg. She commented, even her husband never did that for her. The wine selection was good too. As they were finishing dinner she asked, "How did it go?"

Stumbling through his explanation he finally told Margaret he had proposed to a girl while he was gone, but she had not really accepted because the proposal came from Bob Allen and not Doug Gregory.

Margaret recognized the problem. "When do you think the real Doug Gregory will be able to propose to her?" He said he did not know but was hoping it would not be much longer. "Well, I will miss you when you get married, but I am happy for you. In the meantime, I still have a lot of work to get you ready to be a good husband." He smiled.

The next morning, he told Margaret he did not know what time for her to expect him for the next couple of days. The operation was back on. After she dropped him at the Pentagon, he disappeared for a while. After lunch, he called the restaurant on his Northern Virginia disposable phone and left a message for Jenny. About 6 o'clock she called him back.

Jenny started the conversation off by asking, "What have you been up to?" He told her he had to make a quick business trip to California for the Air Force and just got back. He just wanted to call her and say how much he enjoyed meeting her. Without hesitation she asked, "How about meeting me for a drink?" He told her he would like that and asked what her schedule was. "I am off tonight if you are available." She suggested the bar lounge at the Mayflower Hotel on Connecticut Avenue about eight.

He told her he looked forward to it. Switching to his District cell phone he made a call. All he said was, "This is Waldo. Mayflower. Eight o'clock."

He got to the Mayflower Hotel early and waited on the street. Jenny arrived in a cab, and Greg acted like it was a coincidence they arrived at the same time. He complimented her on her beauty. When they walked into the lobby, everyone seemed to know her. It was almost like she was a queen. Greg thought to himself it must be because of her full-time profession. They were escorted to a table and sofa away from the rest of the people in the lounge. A waiter took their drink order.

Jenny immediately stated asking Greg about his personal life. She asked if he was married and then whether or not he had a girlfriend. Jenny had never seen him in uniform but knew he was a pilot. She asked what kind of airplane he flew. He acted like he was not surprised by the question. He told her he flew the F-22 Raptor before he came to the Pentagon. Before the evening was over, she invited him to go back to her apartment for a nightcap. He declined, saying he had an early start the next morning but looked forward to seeing her.

He asked, "When can I see you again?" She said it depended on her work schedule, but weeknights were better than weekend evenings. She said she would call him when she could look at her work schedule. When they were done negotiating their next "date," he put her in a cab. He then walked to the Metro and headed home.

After his Pentagon stop the next morning, he went to Lewis's office. Lewis told Doug they covered the meeting at the Mayflower. She was probably not wearing a bug. They probably trust her ability to compromise the target. That means we can try to double her on the next date.

A couple of nights later, Jenny called Doug to make another date. They set it up for drinks at the Mayflower Hotel again, the following Monday evening. He told her he was excited to see her again.

In the days between Jenny's call and the next meeting, Doug and Lewis went over the plan in great detail. When the evening came to execute the plan, Doug called the special number on the District disposable phone, simply saying, "Waldo. Mayflower at eight." The operation was on. This time, he arrived at the hotel a few minutes late. He knew an FBI surveillance team would be in the hotel. Letting her arrive before him would give them a chance to see if Jenny might inadvertently acknowledge the presence of anyone she was expecting to be there.

When Doug arrived, he was escorted to the sofa where Jenny was waiting. She was seductively dressed. After a couple of drinks, she said, "Would you like to go back to my place this evening?" He told her that would be great.

Just as they were leaving, there was some traffic confusion right in front of the hotel. An emergency vehicle was blocking the cab stand and the doorman could not get them the next cab in the queue. Just then an empty cab from the street appeared in front of the hotel. The doorman signaled the cab driver he had a pick-up, and he put Doug and Jenny into the cab. Greg reached over to kiss Jenny. When he did, she laid her clutch purse on the seat. He picked it up and stuffed it into a lead lined bag he retrieved from under the driver's seat. The cab then pulled away from the curb and merged into the traffic. She asked what was going on.

Seconds later, Greg said, "Jenny Ling. I am not a captain in the US Air Force. I am an FBI agent and I want to know why you are targeting me." Her immediate response was to deny she was doing any such thing. Greg added, "We know who you are, and based on what you have told me so far, I know you are also working for the Chinese Intelligence Services. You may be about to get yourself into a lot of trouble if you walk away from this opportunity. I want to offer you a chance to avoid being exposed. You are not under arrest, and we are taking you to your apartment. It will take us twenty to twenty-five minutes to get there, and you must make your decision before you get home. You can work for us and tell us all about the other people you have been working for, or we can throw you to the wolves and let the Chinese deal with you."

She sat silent for a few minutes. Then she related she works for the Chinese because she is under duress. She has relatives back in China and is afraid the Chinese will hurt her family if she does not cooperate with them.

Greg added, "Then work for us, too, and we will let you continue your work with the Chinese." She took a deep breath and said she guessed she had no choice.

Once she committed, he told her he needed to ask her a few questions about this evening. "Are you being watched tonight?" She shook her head, no. Do you have a microphone on you so someone can listen to our conversation?" She raised her hand to the side of her face as to indicate she was on a cell phone. "Is there going to be someone back at your apartment to take pictures of us?" She shook her head in the affirmative.

He said, "We're fine. Your phone is in a lead-lined bag on the floor, and no one can hear or get any signals from it while it remains in the bag. When we get to your apartment, I will give you your purse, and we will say good night. If asked, you can deny knowing why your phone didn't work in the cab. You can just tell your handlers I decided I couldn't come in for another drink."

Then Doug told her to wait a few days for instructions. When the cab got to her address, Doug told the driver to wait for him. He then walked her to the apartment building entrance and said, "Sorry I couldn't come in tonight, but I will try harder next time." With that, he kissed her on the cheek and got back in the taxi. It had been a good evening. The cab driver was from the FBI surveillance squad and knew how to shake a tail if there was one. He then drove Doug to Margaret's house.

Margaret was waiting up for him, but this time she had not yet gone to bed. He told her he had already had enough to drink that evening and would stick with water. She got him a glass of water and then asked, "How did it go tonight?"

Doug responded, "It was a ten, but I didn't catch the brass ring." A lipstick smear on his cheek gave it away. She laughed and commented he must have been with the wrong girl tonight. His retort was, "You could say that."

The next day he followed the usual routine, but on the way to meet Lewis, he began to ask himself *how much longer this operation would have to go on.* When he got to the FBI building, he stopped for a minute in the courtyard and just looked at the statute. The inscription on it reads simply, "Fidelity, Bravery, Integrity." It was a good reminder to bring him back into focus. Then he went inside and headed to Lewis's office. Lewis had already seen the reports from the surveillance squad, including the cab driver. He asked Doug how he thought it had gone. Doug told him he thought it had gone as expected. As nearly as he could tell, Jenny Ling was now their double agent.

Lewis indicated it would be a few days before they really knew if she had been successfully recruited. If they were not successful, the operation was blown, and Doug could go back to San Francisco as Bob Allen. The Air Force could send Captain Gregory to some super-secret place until he retires. If they were successful, the Bureau would have to figure out how they want to handle Jenny. All they knew for sure is they had a "swallow" on their hands. The problem is they did not yet know how good a source she would be. Jenny Ling needed to be evaluated before they made an agent assignment or personnel decisions.

Lewis said, "You know more about the scientist back in China than any of us, and what we can get from her about him might tell us how productive she might be. Besides, right now, you are the only person she might trust. I want you to do the eval." Doug wondered how long that might go on. Over the next few days, the Bureau people developed a plan. It involved using another prostitute, who worked with Jenny for the same madame and was a tested Bureau source for criminal matters, as a contact person.

Doug remembered Danny Chen had taken his postgraduate work at the University of Maryland, and Margaret's father had been a professor there. He wondered if their paths had crossed. He asked Lewis to have the FBI research people to check if they could find any connection between the two. After that, it was time to hurry up and wait, again.

About a week later, Lillie, a "lady of the night" who worked with Jenney, approached her in private and told her she had been asked to convey a message. She told Jenny, "I don't know what it is about, and I don't want to know. Please don't ask me why I have been asked to do this. Someone by the name of Doug Gregory wants to meet with you. You tell me when you can meet with him in private, and I will pass it on." Jenny understood exactly what was happening.

Jenny had reported her last date with Captain Gregory to her Chinese handlers, and there had been no repercussions or feedback. She thought to herself, "I guess it is time to fish or cut bait." Since she did not normally "go to work" until the afternoon or evening, the best time to meet him would be in the early morning. She told Lillie to pass the word back she would be available the following Tuesday morning.

In the interim, the FBI research people discovered that Dr. Daniel Chen's dissertation on virology was signed off by Joseph K. O'Brien, PhD. The latter was a research professor and instructor in the Department of Virology, and conducted his research at Fort Detrick, Maryland. A check of Dr. O'Brien's biography indicated he had a daughter, Margaret O'Brien Cassidy.

The message sent back to Jenny through Lillie was on Tuesday morning at 9:30 for Jenny to go to the Hyatt Hotel near the White House. Take the elevator to the second floor, making sure you get on the elevator by yourself. You will be met when you get off the elevator.

When the time came for their meeting, Jenny was right on time. As she got on the elevator, a member of the FBI surveillance squad bumped into a couple of people to make sure no one else got on the elevator with her. When she arrived on the second floor, Doug was there to meet her. He motioned for her to drop her purse in the lead-lined bag he was carrying. He immediately took her to the hotel service elevator, went down to the hotel service area and out a back door. A car was waiting for them. The surveillance team people stayed behind to see if anyone had been following her or tried to find her on the second floor.

Doug and Jenny were driven to a bistro that did not open until the afternoon. There were cooks in the kitchen, but the FBI had an agent sitting outside the private room where Doug interviewed Jenny. The interview was recorded. Doug started by telling Jenny he thought she had made the right decision to cooperate with the FBI. He then wanted to know what she knew about Daniel Chen. She related she did not really know him but had learned some about him from a Colonel Jong, who is the military attaché at the Chinese Embassy. She related she understood Chen had been a student here in the United States and had gotten his doctorate in the study of viruses. When Chen returned to China, he worked for the Wuhan Institute of Virology. According to the Colonel, Chen is credited with developing a virus vaccine, which was smuggled into the US for use by Chinese VIPs during the pandemic.

Doug asked her why she used Chen's name when contacting him? She related she was told if she used Chen's name, he would recognize it, and she could probably set Doug up for a date. Doug asked if she knew why he was a target. She said she did not. Her instructions were just to get Doug in a compromising position so they could photograph him.

Doug then wanted to know a little about Jenny. She told him that she was born and grew up in California. She always wanted to be a dancer and, as a child, studied dance. In high school she was on the dance team. After high school, she moved first to Los Angeles to see if she could get a job in Hollywood as a dancer. She was told movies where they used dancers were no longer being made, and her best chance to find work was on Broadway. She then moved to New York City. During one of her dance try-outs, she sustained an injury which kept her down for quite a while. During the time she could not work she became desperate financially. She was offered a job with an escort service. That is how she got started in what she does now for a living.

Even after she recovered from her accident, she could never really perform as well as a dancer. After a couple of years in New York, she decided she needed to find something else. Her parents had both died, and she did not really want to go back to California. She had visited Washington, DC, and thought it might be a good place to try her luck. A friend in New York gave her a name and telephone number to call in DC. She called the number, and it is where she now works.

While working in New York, she became "professionally" acquainted with a several Chinese diplomats and people who worked for the People's Republic of China at the United Nations. One of the men she had a relationship with was a close friend of Colonel Jong. When she came to Washington, she was introduced to Colonel Jong. He knew about her relatives in China and threatened them unless she would work for him on the side. Doug then wanted to know if Colonel Jong was her handler. She indicated he was not in charge of her assignments, but he is a very important person in the Embassy. She takes instruction from and reports to a woman referred to only as "Lulu."

Special Agent Gregory then asked Jenny about any illegal activities she might be aware of other than her work as a hooker. She said she had never been involved in any other criminal activities, but she occasionally picked up information from the "Johns" who visit the establishment where she works. The one case she remembers most, because it happened in back in July 2016, on the streets of Washington, DC, in the Bloomington neighborhood, was the murder of Seth Rich. He was a twenty-seven-year-old employee of the Democratic National Committee who had access to their computer database. She remembered the police and the media attributed Rich's murder to an ordinary robbery.

What Jenny recalled was her client was a member of the Russian Organized Criminal Group (Bratva) from New York City, who bragged the DNCs computers were hacked by Rich four days before his death, and how the Russians were hired by the DNC to get back the information which Rich had stolen. He had the downloaded information with him on a thumb drive when they shot him. They copied the thumb drive before giving it to their DNC contact, and then sold a copy of the information to Wikileaks. Her client laughed about it because the police and the media got it all wrong. The government and the media tried to say it was connected to the Trump Russian investigation, but that was false information.

Doug was beginning to become concerned about the time. He wanted to know more, but it would have to wait. Her excuse for going to the Hyatt this morning was to meet a new client. He told her the cell phone she has may be bugged, and any conversation or sound around her could be listened to even when it was tuned off. If asked about being out of service this morning, just say, "I didn't know it wasn't working. I didn't get any phone calls."

With that they drove back to the hotel employee entrance, where they were waived in by hotel security with a member of the FBI surveillance team standing next to him. They rode the service elevator up to the second floor, where Doug handed Jenny the purse from the bag. She then went down the guest elevator by herself, and seconds later she was in a cab on the way back to her home.

From the hotel, Doug went straight to the FBI to meet with Lewis, who had already listened to the tape of the interview. Lewis told Doug the surveillance teams have been studying the results of their work, and they do not believe he had been followed after his first visit to the Pentagon. The Chinese were apparently counting on Jenny to trap Doug and were leaving it up to her skills and experience. The only sign the surveillance team had of any other people being involved was a photographer in her apartment building the night of their second date. Now that they have other ways to contact Jenny, it was probably time to have the Air Force Captain Gregory sent on another assignment and get Jenny off the hook trying to trap him.

Lewis's next statement was, "Now what do we do with SA Douglas Gregory? Do we bring him into the Washington Field Office (WFO), do we send him to New York City where we have a lot of Chinese activity, or do we send him back to the San Francisco office as SA Bob Allen?"

Doug saw this as his opening. He told Lewis he had a girlfriend back in California he wanted to marry, but she did not know anything about who he really was. He could not have her marrying a man whose real name she could not take and whose background she knew nothing about. Lewis then said, "Well, we can't keep you in San Francisco using your real name. What do you want to do?" Doug told Lewis he needed some time off to think about his options. Lewis told him to take a couple of days off and come back in the following Monday so they could talk more about it. In the meantime, Lewis would talk to the people in Human Resources (HR) about another assignment.

Doug was not sure it was time to celebrate, but it looked like it was the beginning of something, so why not? He stopped at the wine shop and picked up two bottles of what he hoped would be good reds. He did not care what Margaret had planned for dinner. The main course tonight was Cabernet Sauvignon from Napa. One for Margaret and one for the redhead in San Jose. He decided not to call Blair that evening. He thought it would be best to wait until he had at least a few hours to think about his options. He would call her the next day.

While Margaret fixed dinner and put it on the table, Doug pulled the cork on the first bottle of wine. He poured two glasses, and before they sat down, he offered a toast to Ms. Margaret O'Brien Cassidy. She got a big grin on her face and asked if he had been checking on her.

He responded, "Of course, you don't think I'd sleep with a stranger, do you?"

She answered, "Touché."

When they sat down to eat, he told her it looked like his assignment in DC was coming to an end. They had a major breakthrough, and he was no longer needed. She was a little taken back by the announcement. She knew he could not tell her everything, but she did ask what he would be doing next. He told her he had been given several options but had to think about them.

Doug told her, "I may have to go back to San Francisco before I can decide." She understood he had a proposal to make and the answer he got might be important to his decision.

He told Margaret he was taking a couple of days off from work, and before going back to California, he wondered if there was a chance of having a cup or a drink with Spooky 2. She said she would set it up tomorrow, and maybe they could have a mini reunion the following day. He said he had not turned in his Air Force ID Card and suggested he could just as easily meet them at her office. She said she would let him know in the morning.

Then Doug opened the second bottle of Cab. They adjourned to the living room sofa where he offered a toast "To the girl of my dreams." Margaret thanked him. Doug choked a little on that one, then added, "In California."

Margaret then jested she thought she was the girl of his dreams. Doug, who already probably had too much to drink answered, "You know what I mean. Besides, you are flesh and blood sitting right here. I don't have to dream about you." She smiled and kissed him. The rest of the bottle went undrunk.

The next morning, Margaret called Doug to tell him she had a meeting with Spooky 2 all set up, and for him to come to the Defense Intelligence Agency (DIA) about eleven o'clock. She put him on the DIA Visitors List as Captain Doug Gregory. All he will need is his USAF identification card. Sounded great. A little later in the morning, he called Blair.

When Blair answered the phone, he said, "Good morning. I'm a friend of Bob Allen. Bob and I are making a trip to California in the very near future, and Bob said I should introduce myself to you. Are you ready to meet me?" She indicated she thought so. They then chatted for a few minutes about nothing and everything. Before hanging up, told her he should know more this coming week about when he will be in San Francisco. Doug then decided to take a run in the neighborhood to get his head cleared from the night before, and to think about what was next for him. He also decided to take Margaret out for dinner that evening but without wine.

Late Friday morning, before he had to give up his Air Force ID card, he decided to make one last trip to the Pentagon, to say goodbye to Fort Fumble. From there he took a shuttle to Joint Base Anacostia-Bolling. Checking in at Security, he was given a visitor pass to wear and escorted to the office of Commander Cassidy. She was very circumspect in her greeting. A few minutes later Spooky 2, whose CIA "Nom De Plume" was Kenneth Yang, entered the office. Bob and Yang greeted each other like old lost friends, which they were.

Doug said, "I know you guys live in a world where everyone has a cover name, but it confuses the hell out of me sometimes. My need for a cover has ended, so I can begin using my birth name. Just call me Doug." Yang understood.

At lunch they told each other as much as they could about what, when and where they had been since Monterey. Yang even suggested if Doug ever wanted to change jobs, he knew some people who could get him a job over at The Company (CIA).

Doug said, "Thanks, but I've lived in the world of secret lives long enough." When they were finished, Doug shook Ken's hand and said, "I hope to see you again somewhere." Doug shook Margaret's hand and thanked her for setting up the reunion. He then shuttled back to the Pentagon Station and got on the Orange Line.

It was a quiet weekend at home and a drive in the countryside. He and Margaret spent a long time talking about what was next for both. At school in Monterey, he was her sounding board. Now it was her turn to be his. Doug's plan to marry Blair was not a problem for Margaret. In fact, she looked forward to meeting Blair should the opportunity avail itself. The discussions were more about Doug's options. The advice offered by Margaret was, if Blair accepts his proposal, let her help you make your decision. It will be her life too.

On Monday, Doug was back in Lewis's office. He needed to go back to San Francisco and consult with his intended. Lewis agreed. He told Doug they would take him off special assignment and return SA Robert C. Allen to duty at SFO until he decided what he wanted to do. He and his intended would have a couple of weeks to decide. If he wanted to take a transfer, he would be moved within thirty days after deciding. Doug thought that was a good plan and agreed to it.

He was told to turn in his Air Force ID and Pentagon passes and his FBI credentials issued to Douglas Gregory. He could keep his reissued Ohio driver's license in the name of Douglas Gregory, and other personal identification so he could get married, but as far as the FBI was concerned, he was still Robert Allen as long as he was working in the San Francisco office. He was to report there the following Monday. Until then, he was on annual leave. Robert Allen made a flight reservation for the next afternoon.

Margaret knew he might leave town at any time, so she was not surprised when he told her that evening he was going back to California the very next day. She told him she would miss his companionship but wished him the best of luck.

His reply was, "Hold on to my room for a while. I might be back. She hasn't accepted me yet."

→→ Chapter 12 ←←

On Tuesday, Bob Allen flew to San Francisco, arriving around supper time. By the time he grabbed something to eat and made his way back to his apartment, it was late. He called Blair to say he was home and was anxious to see her. She invited him to come down to San Jose and to stay at her place a couple of days. She had arranged to have the following weekend off.

After working in his apartment on Wednesday morning, Bob drove to San Jose to see Blair. She took off work early to fix her guest a gourmet meal. When Bob showed up, he had a bottle of red Napa Valley wine in his hand. It was a very warm greeting, and Bob felt good about being there.

Blair then asked, "Who am I cooking for tonight? Is it Bob or his friend'? He told her it was both, but he would explain. She responded, "I hope so. The next thing, one of you will want to spend the night with me, and I told you I don't sleep around." Bob laughed.

He helped her put dinner on the table and sat down for one of the best seafood dinners he had ever eaten. The thought running through his mind at the time was *I brought the wrong bottle of wine.* During dinner, he began the story of Douglas Gregory's life, how he came to take a Chinese course in college, about law school after graduation, and then how he came to be in the FBI. Without going into details about finding out from the FBI he had been targeted for recruiting by the Chinese, he said the FBI asked him to go undercover before going through New Agent's Class and language school in Monterey. He said, "That's why you know me as Bob Allen." He explained he was then assigned to the San Francisco office because it is one of the four offices where they have the greatest need for Mandarin speakers. He skipped over the kind of cases he worked. When the Chinese made a surreptitious inquiry about Douglas Gregory, the Bureau decided to try to find out why.

They could not have SA Robert Allen involved in investigating a matter about Douglas Gregory because he could be identified as being one in the same. Instead, they put the real Douglas Gregory out there as bait. When the Chinese took the bait, the FBI had what they wanted, and Doug no longer needed his cover as Bob Allen. After that he could go back to being SA Doug Gregory, but that presented a whole set of other problems. What to do with Bob Allen? The FBI could not just replace Allen with Gregory in the same office.

So now Blair Reed knew who Bob's "friend" was. The question now was, did she want to marry a man she technically just met? Of course, that was a stupid question, but she knew she would always be accused of marrying the best friend of a man she had been dating.

She then said, "I have a question. What was your nickname in high school?"

As the evening grew on the discussion turned to the other problems they would have to deal with. Blair reminded him, "You know I am going to be the mother of two boys. Are you ready for that?" Doug said he was.

She then asked, "Where will we live?"

While he could move to San Jose, he could not go back to work for the FBI in San Francisco as Doug Gregory. He was not enamored with keeping his cover name. They agreed none of this had to be decided that night. Bob's friend decided he would not propose to Blair that evening, and she did not suggest she would now marry him even though she now knew who he was.

She went back to work the next day, and he went back to San Francisco to get ready for the weekend. He worried she might surprise him and still say no. Blair was a strong woman and made her own decisions. She had good job, was prepared to be a single mother of two boys, and apparently had the finances to survive without getting married. He would have to wait, at least until the weekend, to find out.

Blair arrived in San Francisco on Friday evening, still dressed in her work attire. He had dinner waiting for her. Very little was said by either that evening about any decisions. It was just time to relax and get reacquainted. The next morning Doug asked Blair if she wanted to go with him while he ran a very important errand. If he had to go someplace, she was not going to stay by herself. Doug then took her back to Baker Beach, reputed to be the most romantic spot in the Golden Gate city.

Doug then asked her to walk on the beach with him. Once there he kissed her and asked, "Ms. Reed, I love you very much. Will you marry me?" Before she could even answer, he reached in his pocket and pulled out a small ring box. In it was rather large solitaire green diamond engagement ring he had purchased from a diamond merchant in Washington, DC. While she was expecting the proposal, she was stunned by both the size and color of the diamond. It was perfect for a beautiful woman with red hair.

Her response was, "Yes, Douglas Gregory, I will marry you. You're a good man, and I also love you very much." With that he put the ring on her finger. It was a perfect fit. She admired the color of the diamond again and added, "You're the only man I know who would think of something like this."

Decisions about their future had not been resolved. After a lovely engagement lunch, they went back to Doug's apartment. She said, "I need to tell you a couple of things about my situation we never got around to discussing. I told you about the family trust my parents lived off. When they died, I became the beneficiary of the trust. Also, I have a very good salary at Google, and I have managed to invest well. We should be able to live reasonably well wherever we live and whatever we decide to do." Blair added she really did not want to stay at Google. She has had other opportunities, and since Shirley's death, she has been considering leaving the company and just becoming the mother of the twins.

Doug told Blair, while he enjoyed San Francisco and his work there, he did not want to continue working under a pseudo name even if it meant moving somewhere else. Of course, the three most likely assignments for him were New York City, Boston, or Washington, DC.

Blair said, "I prefer not to raise the boys in New York City." Doug understood. Everything had been decided except when and where they would get married. On that they would have to roll with the punches a little, knowing things were probably going to happen fast now.

After the weekend Bob Allen went back to work in the San Francisco. When asked, he told his ASAC the special assignment went well, but he was glad to be back. He was not sure what else to say. All his cases had been reassigned to other special agents in his absence, except his SI sources. Contacting them would be a good place to start and see if there was anything going on in the intel world.

He contacted Chen Fang to let him know he was leaving San Francisco, and someone else would be in contact with him. Chen was glad to see Bob and told him about a discussion he had overheard while listening to the old men in the store talk. They were talking about Chinese involvement in the upcoming presidential election in the United States. Apparently, the Chinese had developed a computer-hacking ability, which would allow them to access certain voting machines in the US, when they are connected to the internet, and to change votes to the other candidate. This was accomplished in real time while the votes were being cast or tallied and was done running in background, so it would not be apparent to anyone looking at the votes as they are cast. Using VPN technology, the Chinese could make the hacks, if discovered, look like they are coming from European countries. While the 2020 election was still some time off, this information was reported immediately to the Bureau.

Now that Doug and Blair had a chance to talk and make some decisions, he called Lewis at the SOG and let him know what they had decided. He told Lewis about their plans to get married, and he wanted to drop the cover name, even it meant leaving San Francisco. He mentioned his intended had two young children she was responsible for and did not want to raise them in the Big Apple. Also, he would like to take some leave between transfers, if possible. Lewis reminded him he would likely be brought back to Washington, DC, and assigned to a Chinese squad in the Washington field office (WFO). Doug said that an assignment to WFO would be fine. Doug knew it was not up to him. He was no longer a protected special person controlled by the NSB people. He would just have to wait to see what the HR branch wanted to do with him. Lewis said he would work on it.

It did not take long. Within a few days of the conversation with Lewis, SA Robert C. Allen received a letter, telling him he was being transferred to the SOG. At the same time, SA Douglas Gregory received a separate letter advising him he was being assigned to WFO. There were three weeks in between Allen's departure date from SF and Gregory's reporting date at WFO.

Chapter 13

Once Doug got his assignment, Blair called the shots on their planning. She decided they should get married in San Jose where she could have a few guests from Google and a couple of her girlfriends from college. Neither Blair nor Doug has spent anytime seeing the United States. Their honeymoon would be a leisurely trip across country in her SUV, with a stop in Texas to see their new sons. Once they were in DC, they would stay in a short-term residence apartment while Blair scoured the area for a home. Her boys were not going to be raised in an apartment building, not if she could help it.

They were married as Mr. and Mrs. Douglas Gregory, in the sanctuary of Westminster Presbyterian Church in San Jose, attended by twenty friends and acquaintances of Blair, including a couple of senior executives from Google, one of whom gave the bride away. Dr. Reed was well connected and obviously a favorite of the people at the company who knew her.

They arrived in the Washington, DC, just as the COVID-19 virus was declared a pandemic. Everyone was wearing masks, and the government was issuing conflicting directives. Much of it appeared to be intentional disinformation from the media, which was using the pandemic to *control* the narrative.

They moved into a temporary apartment residence in Northern Virginia. Doug reported to the WFO and was assigned to the Chinese squad. Nobody had checked on him by calling anyone in San Francisco, but Doug knew all the right people in the San Francisco office, and he came with a good recommendation. He was no longer a first office agent, so he was accepted by his peers in WFO as somebody who knew what he was doing. When he checked the Bureau indices, he found the contact with Jenny Ling had not been reassigned to anyone else. He was also assigned a couple of other SI sources, which had previously been worked by a special agent, now retired. This would keep him busy for a while.

In the meantime, Blair was busy planning for their time in DC. She made contact with a recommended real estate broker, began checking on schools for the boys, and a country club where she could play golf. At night, she turned into a gourmet chef. She settled in fast.

It was not long after they arrived in Washington, she got a telephone call from the Democrat National Committee (DNC). They had been given her name by someone from Google, who described her as a talented individual they might want to hire or use as a volunteer. Blair told the caller she had just moved to DC and was not yet ready to go to work full time but might be able to volunteer some time. She would have to talk to her husband first. The caller gave her a name and a call back number.

At dinner that evening Blair told Doug about the call from the DNC. He said, "We never really talked about politics, but I am surprised you are a Democrat. I thought you were more conservative than that."

Blair told him while she was in college, she did not think much about politics, but when she went to Google, she was advised to register to vote as a Democrat. She was told the Dems control politics, even when the Republicans are in office, and if she wanted to move ahead at Google, she would best be a registered Democrat. Since she did not have any real interest in party politics, she did what was suggested, but when she voted, she voted for the best candidate regardless of party. Doug told her he was registered as an independent, but when it came to voting, he voted the same way. If she wanted to do some volunteer work at the DNC, it was up to her.

Through SA Amos Teasley, the criminal squad agent who had Lillie as a source, Doug arranged another meeting with Jenny. Doug was no longer worried about the Chinese trying to compromise him, but he wanted to make sure Jenny was not identified as a source. His first meeting with Jenny since he returned to DC was in the back room of a friendly ladies clothing store. He wanted to know if Jenny had any problems because of his not going back to her apartment. She indicated she had not.

Doug then asked for her to tell him about Colonel Jong. She said she hates him, but she is afraid to cross him. He regularly abuses her. Doug wanted to know if he ever talks to her about what he does at the Embassy. She told Doug he talks about the fact he has several Chinese American friends he drinks with and who go places for him where he is not permitted to travel—mostly to military installations. As far as she knows she has not met any of the people who do things for him. Another of his drinking friends he likes to talk about is the Chinese first assistant cultural attaché, who Jong once identified as their intelligence chief of station.

Doug then asked if Lulu has been tasking her? She indicated she had been tasked, but she did not know as much about the targets as she did Captain Gregory. Doug thought it was time to bypass Lillie as a go-between for future meetings. They set up another way Jenny could reach out to him when she had some information and a signal he could set for when he needed to reach her.

Over the next few days Doug also set out making initial contact with his other newly assigned SIs. He also covered a couple of leads from the San Francisco office. Since the leads from San Francisco were covered by SA Douglas Gregory, who they never heard of in San Francisco, they had no way of knowing it was the work of SA Bob Allen.

One of the SIs Doug inherited was middle-aged man who ran an independent IT business. His customers included a couple of restaurants and other small businesses in Washington's Chinatown. Since he had worked in the community for a long time, he was trusted by most if not all of them. As a result, he had been contacted by at least two employees of the Chinese Embassy to do work on the computers of family members. Occasionally, he would find something on one of the computers, which was probably added accidently. Recently he noticed the name of a person at the DNC, which seemed out of place. He wondered why someone at the Chinese Embassy would be in contact with someone at the DNC. He had not made a copy of what was on the computer, but he did write down the name of the person at the DNC.

Blair and Doug decided on a house on in Oakton, Virginia. It was a four-bedroom, three-bath house on two acres of land. Both were anxious to get away from apartment living. It was a beautiful piece of property and would be perfect for the boys. Blair started purchasing furniture as soon as they signed the contract, and they moved in the day after they closed on the purchase.

Blair had contacted a few of the club pros at some of the local country clubs. When they found out she had a three handicap, they were all anxious to have her play their course. Several of them arranged with club members for her to play as a guest in a lady's foursome.

Being uncertain about what to say about her husband's work, she just passed herself off as a young, retired executive from Google. At dinner, she shared with her husband the information about the women she met and their husbands. They were some of the creme de la creme of Washington Society.

Occasionally, the dinner conversation would go back to some of the experiences Blair had with Google. She fretted over the fact that Big Tech companies always seemed to be trying to either gobble up their competition or somehow put them out of business. They did this in several ways. They collected data on everything and everybody, but they did not always share all the pertinent data with businesses they were trying to eliminate or acquire. They were politically involved in order to garner favoritism, to the extent they sometimes interfered with a political adversary's messaging or interest. What they were doing was intentionally trying to change the landscape of the country. Blair did not think what they were doing was for the best. The key words by which these woke companies seemed to live by were *control* and *power*.

Doug did not have much to talk about in the evenings, since a lot of his work was classified. He did suggest, since there is a lot of corruption in government in Washington, there are a lot of people who are apparently not very fond of the FBI. He told her, if it was not particularly important for someone to know what her husband did for a living, to just tell them he is an import-export specialist for the government. After all, that is exactly what he does. He imports information and then exports it.

Doug had not been in touch with Margaret Cassidy since he returned to Washington, DC. He hesitated to call her, since he had previously been involved with her, but she could still be an important contact for him. Besides, it would not be good if Margaret found out from someone else he was back in town. He explained to Blair who Margaret was, his past relationship with her, and the importance of keeping her as a contact since they were both involved with the Chinese world. Blair told him she knew he was probably seeing someone when he was here on special assignment, but so long as he understood that all changed when he married her, he was free to contact Commander Cassidy. Doug told Blair that at one time Margaret had even said she would like to meet her.

Blair told her husband, "If you want me to meet her, I'm up to it." Doug thought that might be a good idea. It would make it easier to converse with Margaret occasionally and not create a problem at home.

When he called Margaret, his first words were, "I'm back, but don't save my room." She knew exactly what he was saying.

Her response was to congratulate him. He then went on to explain he was permanently transferred from San Francisco to the Washington field office, and he had abandoned his cover. Before leaving California, he married Blair, she left her job, and they were now living here in Virginia. Margaret commented he had been busy.

Doug told her, "I want you to meet my bride. I have told her all about you, and she is willing to meet." Margaret suggested Sunday brunch some weekend. Doug thought that would be fine and told her he would get back to her in a couple of days.

Over the summer, the presidential election had been heating up. There were no serious challengers to President Trump for renomination to a second term. The Democrat field of seventeen had winnowed down to just two candidates. Misinformation about the candidates and what they stood for abounded. Money was choosing up sides. The electorate seemed to be supporting the incumbent president, but even some of his party leaders seemed lukewarm about his candidacy. The opposition was in lockstep and agreed to support whoever their party chose. The Democrats finally selected former Vice President Joe Biden as their candidate, and his campaign was run almost entirely by surrogates. It was unlike any election season the US had seen in over one hundred years. The race appeared to be one sided, but the Democrats remained confident of victory. It was almost like they knew they had a lock on the election.

Blair received another telephone call from the DNC. This time it was a high-level party official whose wife Blair recently played golf with. He obviously had checked with someone at Google. He knew too much about her background to not to have checked on her. Strangely enough, he did not mention her husband. Since Blair married Doug on the way out the door at Google, not many knew much about her husband. The caller also knew Blair had previously been called about a job at the DNC. This time she was invited to lunch to discuss it. She thought it might be fun, and it was getting a little warm in the summer to play much golf.

She accepted the lunch invitation. The interview at lunch went well. Given her computer background and corporate management experience, they talked about her helping in data management. When asked about her husband's work, she used the line about him being an import-export specialist for the government. Her luncheon host probably though her husband worked for the Department of Commerce, but what difference did it make? She was only a volunteer, not applying for a real job.

Doug, Blair, and Margaret were finally able to get together for Sunday brunch. It was an easy introduction as both Blair and Margaret were sophisticated women and neither exhibited any sign of jealously. Blair had what she wanted, and Margaret could always find a man to take care of her.

The girls hit it off, and it was a very friendly meeting. Blair remembered that Shirley had actually met the language class members back in Monterey, and that Margaret would have known about Doug's relationship with Shirley. Given that, Blair told Margaret about Shirley getting married back in Texas, about her twins, and the death of both parents. She went on to mention now that they had a place for the twins, she and Doug were going to adopt the boys. Margaret said, "Can I be their aunt?"

Before going to work at the DNC, Doug gave Blair the name of a person he wanted his wife to be careful talking to. He did not tell her it was a person an SI had identified as being in touch with the Chinese Embassy. He told her just do not discuss his work. Conversations with that person should be one sided. Just be a listener.

On Monday, Blair went to work as a volunteer in the offices of the DNC. Because of her job history, she was assigned to help in the office of the chief technology officer (CTO). She would be working with the director of data, the data acquisitions manager, the data services manager and a host of engineers and software specialist. For now, "until she learned the ropes," she would just be kind of gopher for anyone who needed help. Blair thought that would be fine. At dinner, she reported to her husband the day had been uneventful, and she had been well received. She had been introduced to the lady whose name Doug had given her. She is a special assistant to the CTO, responsible for coordinating all technology and data matters. Her husband is a "K Street lobbyist" who represents a couple of Big Teach companies and a few companies from China.

Doug kept his Northern Virginia disposable cell phone, since it did not appear to have been compromised, to set up meetings with Jenny. He got a call from her one evening, asking for a morning meeting the next day. As previously planned, they met in a quiet breakfast restaurant near where she lived. It was already late morning, and people were not eating out as much because of the COVID-19 rules and mask requirements. They had the restaurant almost to themselves, and they asked to be seated away from everyone else. Jenny told him she had been with Colonel Fong the evening before, and after a few drinks, he started talking about how the Chinese were working with companies in America to fix the election in favor of Joe Biden. They were only targeting five key states. So, it would not look so obvious, the Chinese were not working on the state or congressional races. They even had contacts in the DNC Headquarters.

Doug told Blair there was problem at the DNC, but not to stick her nose into it trying to find out what was going on. He said, "You are not a spy. Just keep your eyes open and listening to what is going on. If you find anything you think is a bit unusual talk to me about it before going to anyone else." Blair understood and agreed to be careful. Blair was not aware of the Chinese plan to interfere with the upcoming presidential election. Doug had not discussed it with her.

What Blair brought home was information Big Tech was helping the Democrats by censoring Tweets and posts supporting President Trump, and they were promoting posts which favored Joe Biden. Also, during the election, some of the companies would be involved in moving election-day results electronically to tabulation center servers in Europe. The European servers would then consolidate the voting results and feedback false information to the US media for distribution as the polls closed in the eastern states. This was especially important in the swing states since the polls would still be open in some of those states and in Arizona and Nevada. It was understood the tabulation centers in Europe would not accurately represent the actual vote. The totals would be changed in favor of Joe Biden.

The doctored information could be used to represent a Biden victory. The idea being undecided voters would then vote for Biden and Trump supporters might stay home. The Democrats needed those states. She also learned one of the European companies tabulating this information was Scytl, a Spanish company with a tabulation center in Germany, owned by George Soros.

The people she worked for at the DNC quickly learned Blair was very smart. Since there was no reason to distrust her loyalty, they began allowing her to have access to more data and to some policy decision-making. It became very clear to her the "method in their madness" was to maintain control of everything they were involved in. Particularly the information which was generated by Big Tech. It helped the Fourth Estate was complicit and compliant.

Chapter 14

Blair got word from Texas the twins were now available for adoption. She and Doug immediately made their arrangements to fly to Austin to pick up the boys and to bring them home. It was an exciting time for both. Blair looked forward to being a mom. After the adoption hearing, she commented to Doug, "I am glad I am married to their father and that we are all together." Doug was not sure how his wife meant the statement, since it could be interpreted two ways, but it really did not make any difference. He was now a proud father of twin boys and the husband of a wonderful wife, the most beautiful redhead in Washington, DC and Northern Virginia. It could not get any better.

After the adoption, Blair gave up here volunteer work at the DNC but agreed to remain available for consultation if she could help. It was still several weeks until the November election. The next thing she had to do was introduce the boys to Aunt Margaret. On the weekend following their return from Texas, she had Margaret over to meet Robert and Charles Gregory. Margaret immediately dubbed the two Bobby and Charley, giving each one a Naval Academy blanket for their beds and a treasure trove of toys. You could tell she missed having children, but she had a wonderful time playing aunt.

Blair loved being a mother, doting on her children. Weather permitting, she would take the boys out for a ride in the double stroller every day. She carried on conversations with them like they were adults. They were both very responsive to the stimuli around them and appeared to be happy babies. If Blair had to go somewhere, she would tuck the boys safely in the back seat of her SUV, in the best toddler seats she could buy. Doug was also a good parent, but he was a busy father during the week and sometimes on weekends.

The COVID-19 pandemic was spreading both in the United States and around the world. China was still denying responsibility for the virus and was being supported by the World Health Organization (WHO). Doug's sources were beginning to report more about the virus having been created in the Wuhan laboratory, and the real reason for its release: China could exert more *control* and *power* over world events. The virus would create havoc for China's political and economic competitors as they attempted to stem the virus, while the Chinese continued their quest to carry out China's Dream.

Information was also beginning to surface that part of the Wuhan lab, under the direction of a Dr. Daniel

Chen, had developed a vaccine to protect those involved in working with the virus. It is important to note there were no reported deaths of people who worked in the Wuhan lab. Prior to the outbreak in the US in January 2020, some of the Chinese vaccine had been smuggled into the US for important Chinese people living here. The vaccine could not be brought into the US legally without disclosure of its purpose, and the Chinese did not want the world to know there was a vaccine for the virus. This would explain the illegal shipment SA Bob Allen picked up on in October 2018.

The US was struggling mightily to develop vaccines to combat the spread of the COVID-19 virus. The president had implemented parts of the Defense Production Act to encourage drug companies to research and produce the vaccines. It was paid for by the advance purchase of millions of doses of yet undeveloped vaccines. Under a program called "Operation Warp Speed" the first vaccines in the US were tested, approved, and mass produced within nine months of the first outbreak of the virus. The US accomplished something which had never before been achieved anywhere in the world, with the possible exception of the vaccine produced in China.

Doug's sources were also reporting more information on the Chinese interest and participation in the upcoming election. Most of the actual hacking and implementation of programs to infer with election results would be done in China or outside the United States, using the internet. The exception would be the use of foreign made software specifically created to alter election results and sold to voting machine companies for use in their equipment. All of this was likely the work of the Chinese Ministry of State Security (MSS). While how this was being accomplished was the responsibly of the National Cyber Investigative Joint Task Force (NCIJTF), it was often information from FBI field offices human intelligence sources which gave the NCIJFT leads to follow.

While the nation was hyped on Election Day, for Doug it was almost anti-climactic. He voted before going to work in the morning, and Blair went to the polls when Doug came home. After dinner, they got the boys ready for bed, and the parents sat down for an evening of television election results. For the first time, Doug said something about how he expected the presidential race to turn out.

Doug told Blair, "The word on the street is that the election has been fixed, and Biden will be the winner."

She knew his reference to "the street" meant he probably had some kind of inside information. When asked why he said that he went on to explain, "China and possibly several other countries were trying to change the election outcome by changing the vote count in key states. China needs to get rid of President Trump. Trade negotiation for them was a disaster, and four more years of dealing with a Trump administration would severely interfere with their economic plans. The Trump response to the spread of the COVID-19 virus was handled better than China had expected. The US is not backing down in response to China's military buildup in the South China Sea. Basically, Trump has stalled or at least slowed China's progress toward control of the world economy. China does not want to fight a land or nuclear war with the US They do not feel they need to. They are trying to weaking the government by selecting its leaders, who will negotiate what the Chinese want."

As the election results began coming in, it was rather obvious something was afoot. The election landslide Trump supporters were predicting, based on his campaign popularity, was not happening. The apparent support for Biden's election was enough to keep him in the race until the five key swing states were reported. Television watchers, who did not stay up, went to bed not knowing who the next president was going to be. When they awoke in the morning, it was projected by all the media outlets that Joe Biden had won the election. Trump refused to concede defeat.

It was then allegations of mass voter fraud began to surface in the news. Trump supporters called for recounts and investigations. Biden supporters branded the Republicans as sore losers and called for the Trump supporters to put it behind them. Numerous lawsuits were filed to overturn the results in the swing states.

Experts and voting fraud investigators took to the airways to explain the anomalies that occurred. Denials abounded. The media took sides. If there was a problem, the time for the courts to fix it was insufficient to do it before states had to certify their election results and the Electoral College met to confirm the results. Judges, without the opportunity to hear any evidence, simply dismissed the lawsuits. Even the Supreme Court of the United States (SCOTUS) refused to weigh in on the election results. It was fait accompli. Joseph Biden was deemed to be the forty-sixth president of the United States, and he was inaugurated on January 20, 2021.

The Chinese plan to concentrate only on the presidential election was borne out by the results of the races in the House of Representative and the US Senate. There did not appear to be any major change of votes in those other races. The Democrats already had a sizable majority in the House and were expected to continue their control. In the end, they would up losing nine seats but maintained their majority. The Republicans lost two Senate seats in a special election after the presidential election but kept fifty seats. The result of having Biden in the White House, the Democrats maintaining their majority in the House, and there being equal representation in the Senate was that the Democrats seized control of the federal government. Because of US Senate rules, the power of the Democrats was still not complete, but they were clearly in control.

→→→ Chapter 15 ←←←

There were no major changes at the FBI after President Biden's election. Shortly after the inauguration, the president announced he would be keeping Christopher Wray as the director. Even though the Bureau was continuing to suffer from the outfall of their handling of the Russia-Russia Hoax and related investigations, the public seemed to still support the FBI. The outstanding issues surrounding those investigations now seem to be headed to Senate hearings. There an equally divided Senate, along with a tie-breaking vote by the Democrat vice president, the investigations could be buried. Politics inside the Beltway seemed to be almost back to normal after four years of Trump's leadership.

The normal season of presidential administration personnel changes was underway. All the government's Plum Book positions were up for grabs. Of course, Cabinet and White House positions would be filled first. Then came some of the second-level positions. Other high-level staff positions in the Departments and Agencies, some of which require Senate confirmation, and some do not, would be filled in due course.

About a week after Biden moved into the White House, Margaret called Doug to say she might be reassigned. The White House was specifically looking for a Field Grade Naval Officer who spoke Chinese to fill a vacancy on the staff of the National Security Council (NSC). She was about due for reassignment anyway, and she met the qualifications for the position. NAVPERS had recommended her. She would know any day.

Aunt Peggy was quickly becoming part of the Gregory family. On weekends, she was always at Doug and Blair's home, playing with and looking after the twins. They were beginning to enjoy her too. When she came over, she usually had twin matching outfits for the boys or some kind of educational toy. She was in her realm. Blair would sometimes use the occasion to run to the grocery store or to hit a few balls at the driving range. It was nice having Margaret around.

Occasionally Doug would preempt the activities Blair and Margaret had planned for Bobby and Charley. They were both very active boys, and Doug liked to pack them in his car and take them to a nearby park. The COVID-19 virus was keeping everyone at home most of the time. It was a chance to get the boys out of the house a little more.

After the election, things started picking up for Doug's squad. When Biden served as vice president under Barack Obama, he was responsible for handling relations with China. Biden made several trips to China during his tenure as VP and met with Xi Jinping on each occasion. On some of these government trips aboard

Air Force Two, he was accompanied by his son, Robert Hunter Biden. Hunter's first visit to China was in 2010 during his father's first term as vice president. The vice president's son's presence on these trips received little public attention. The media covered the official visit of the VP, but Hunter seldom was present for any official events or meetings. Information about the nature of the vice president's son working personal business on these government trips was just now starting to be reported by FBI and other intelligence sources.

Hunter Biden was trained in the law, had worked in the hedge fund industry, and had been a banker, a lobbyist, and a public administration official. He knew his way around political circles and was the son of the vice president. He had a lot to offer the Chinese, and they were ready to exploit the opportunity. Meeting government officials and others involved in promoting Chinese interests, Hunter was soliciting money in exchange for influence. Over the period his father was VP and even later, the Chinese gave millions of dollars to companies and investment organizations which Biden either owned or was involved in. The quid pro quo was not just for a direct return on their investment. It was more for the promise of opportunities, which might otherwise be denied to the Chinese.

While some of China's opportunities were limited during the Trump administration, they were willing to make the investment for the future. After all they were actively engaged in efforts to make sure Trump was not reelected. What gave the Chinese even more confidence was the fact they were assured "the Big Guy" was going to receive ten percent of whatever the Chinese gave Hunter. Shortly after intelligence sources started learning about Hunter's financial involvement with the Chinese, some conservative media organizations and individual investigative reporters began reporting these same facts.

The news about Hunter Biden's trading with China on his father's name and position was not really something new. Prior to the election, similar allegations had surfaced about his involvement in the Ukraine. At the time, Vice President Joe Biden was the Obama administration's point man with Ukraine. With no experience in the gas business, Hunter Biden obtained a position on the board of directors with Burisma, which was under investigation by Ukraine authorities. While everyone seemed to wonder about Joe Biden's role in all this, the media was willing to give him a pass.

One evening when Doug came through the door, he was surprised to see the dining room table all set up for supper. Usually, they ate their family meals in the kitchen. There were flowers on the table and two highchairs at the table too. He thought he must have missed some important date. He walked into the kitchen where Blair was working on dinner and gave her a kiss. Before giving the boys their hug and kiss, he asked Blair, "Am I in trouble? Did I forget something?" She smiled and told him not exactly.

When they sat down to the table the conversation turned to her activities for the day. She related she had gone to the doctor that morning and then announced, "It appears I am a couple of months pregnant. I thought we ought to celebrate."

Doug got up from the table to give her another kiss. He knew it was too early to tell if it was going to be a boy or a girl, so he just told the boys, "It looks like you guys will soon have to share with another sibling." Then all kinds of questions started going through Doug's mind, but this was not the time to ask them. They would all be answered over the next few months.

When Aunt Peggy came over the following weekend, she commented on how Blair seemed to have a glow to her. Blair told her it was probably because she was pregnant. Margaret was elated. Now she was going to be an aunt to three children. The announcement was just in time for their first Christmas together as a family. Margaret wanted to know if she was buying blue or pink for Christmas. Blair said she wish she knew, but for now anyone's guess was as good as hers.

Because of the COVID-19 restriction, there was no office Christmas party for the Washington field office. Doug purchased a tree for their living room, enough lights to cover it, and a few ornaments. He and Blair had both saved a few special ornaments from their childhood. They decided instead of loading it down with a bunch of store-bought stuff, they would just add special meaning ornaments each year. Of course, the boys loved the tree lights.

Christmas Eve was a quiet evening. Church services had been cancelled because of the pandemic. Margaret was alone, so she was invited to spend the night with them. They enjoyed an excellent meal, and Doug and Margaret shared a bottle of wine. Blair stayed with sparkling water. Before retiring, Doug reminded Margaret, he hoped she brought something to wear to bed. He did not need her wandering around the house in her usual sleeping attire. He offered to loan her a pair of pajamas, but she said she brought a nightgown and robe for overnight.

Santa Claus came after everyone went to bed. In the morning, Blair brought the boys in to see what was under the tree. It looked Santa must have come in a truck rather than a sleigh. The gifts from Santa were all unwrapped. The boys were very excited. The three adults gave wrapped gifts to each other. Doug had purchased a pair of green diamond earrings for Blair, to match her diamond engagement ring. Blair gave Doug a pair of gold FBI cufflinks to wear with the French cuff shirts he liked. Doug and Blair gave Margaret a silver charm bracelet with a charm from each of the boys. Christmas Day was otherwise uneventful. Margaret played with the boys, but they tired. By their nap time, she decided to call it a day. In the evening, things seemed to be getting back to normal, so Blair and Doug spent the evening relaxing. Doug thought maybe now would be a good time to ask some of his questions about their baby she was carrying.

Doug's first question, right out of the box, was "Have you thought of any names yet?"

Blair indicated she had thought some about names, but since they did not yet know whether it was going to be a boy or a girl, she had not given it any real thought. They talked about family names and some of the traditional first names but were not enthused about any of them.

Then Doug said, "I have one I want you to consider." Blair asked what it was. He said, "Reed." She wanted to know why her maiden name. His answer, "It's a name for either a boy or a girl. I like having it as a name in the family and it is appropriate." She asked what he meant by appropriate. He explained, "The derivation of the name Reed is from the Old English word 'read,' meaning 'red.' It was used as a nickname for someone with red hair before becoming a surname." She was amazed at his knowledge about this and suggested since they had some time before they had to make a decision they put it on the list of possibilities.

The period between Christmas and New Year's Eve continued to be filled with allegations of voter fraud in the presidential election, about the development and distribution issues plaguing the coronavirus vaccine, and about Hunter Biden's problems. It did not portend for the kind of New Year everyone was looking forward to. Even the Time Square celebration in New York City was cancelled, except for a silly appearance by Mayor

Bill de Blasio. The nation celebrated New Year's Eve mostly on television.

New Year's Day was on a Friday, so it was a long weekend to recover from nothing. Doug was glad to get back to work the following Monday morning. His squad was called in for a security briefing. The genesis of the briefing was that the powers to be were expecting a lot of trouble in the District over the next few weeks, at least through the Inauguration on January 20. Agents were instructed to contact their informants and sources as quickly as possible about information regarding planned terrorism. All leave was cancelled and agents in WFO were told to plan on working every day through the inauguration. The biggest problem days were likely to be when Congress meets as the Electoral College on January 6, and for the inauguration on January 20. Agents will be given specific assignments on those days.

Doug immediately set out a signal for Jenny to call him. She did, and they set up a meeting. Of course, all these meetings began with a "how are you" question. Jenny told him she had been very busy over the holidays. She said the new politicians coming to town were eager to visit where she worked. They had a lot of money to throw around and did not seem to be concerned about the "no kissing" restriction that was imposed because of the COVID-19 pandemic.

When she finished, he asked her if she had heard anything about any planned violence in DC over the next several weeks. She related a lot of the "Johns" who visited her establishment talked about it. She heard a protest was planned at the Capitol on January 6, following President Trump's rally at the National Mall in the morning. While some Trump supporters planned to march to the Capitol after his speech to stage a peaceful protest, terrorist groups were being recruited to join the protest and to create havoc at the Capitol. She did not know which groups were planning to join the protest, but there was more than one.

They then moved on to other information she had picked up on. Colonel Jong was as proud as a peacock China had gotten Joe Biden elected. The cultural attaché, who works for the MSS, had told Jong they successfully changed enough votes in the five swing states to make the difference. With what they had on Hunter and Joe Biden, dealing with the US on trade issues, military control of the South China Sea shipping lanes, and other issues would be "a piece of cake." Since the Biden administration had announced plans to rejoin the World Health Organization, and WHO was still firmly in Chinese control, the Chinese were beginning to think they had the issue of fault for the spread of COVID-19 behind them.

Doug made the rounds of several of his other sources and picked up a similar information, but none was as good as Jenny Ling. She had an advantage few other sources had.

Back in the office the FBI Agents and support staff began preparing for their special assignments on

Wednesday, January 6. Since there was no indication of any local Chinese people or gangs being involved in the planned protest Doug's assignment would be "generic," with no coat and tie, and no FBI ball cap or blue raid jacket. His job would be to dress like a marcher, join the crowd, and march to the Capitol to identify anyone in the march who might be a not so peaceful protestor. While he would be armed, as FBI agents always are, his principal "weapon" for the day would be a camera.

Instead of attending the rally near the White House, Doug joined the protestors just outside the Capitol. When it appeared some of the crowd at the Capitol were not necessarily peaceful protestors and were entering the Capitol itself, he decided to go inside too. The Capitol police were trying to keep the protestors out of the building, but they were being overwhelmed. Doug showed his FBI badge to one of the police officers and was allowed to go inside.

In the Capitol rotunda, one protestor approached Doug and asked him if he was from the press. Doug indicated he was not. The protestor then wanted to know why Doug was taking pictures of the protestors. Doug said, "Just for the hell of it." The protestor took a swing at and hit him. Doug then dropped the protestor with one punch. A Capitol police officer saw the whole incident and was immediately on the scene. Doug flashed his FBI badge again. The officer told Doug he would take care of the protestor. The policeman knew this was not an incident to be reported. If reported it would probably result in a Congressional investigation and charges of abuse by the FBI. Doug moved on.

The people inside the Capitol were restless. Some of the violent protestors entered Congressional offices, and others got onto the floor of the House of Representatives. The Secret Service had to rescue Vice President Mike Pence who was sitting as the presiding officer of the Electoral College. The Capitol police herded the members of Congress into a secure area until the building could be cleared. Over 300 people were arrested, one died from being shot by a Capitol policeman, and four others died from other injuries. The one thing was clear: because of the distance between the National Mall and the Capitol, the size of the crowd in the streets, few if any of the marchers who were at the president's rally could have even reached the Capitol by the time the riot was in progress. The riot at the Capitol was not a spontaneous event. Someone planned it. The Electoral College did not complete its work until late into the night, and nobody from WFO went home until it was over.

The two-week period between the Electoral College and the inauguration were an "all hands-on deck" time for the agents from WFO and all other law enforcement agencies in the District. The mayor demanded the District be locked down, fencing was put up around the Capitol, and National Guard troops were brought in from several states. The chief of police of the Capitol police resigned. The Speaker of the House and the new Majority Leader of the Senate were visible but ineffective.

The Departments of Defense and the Army disclaimed responsibility. Everyone passed the buck. Nobody knew who was in charge or claimed responsibility for turning Washington, DC, into an armed camp. It was clear President Trump, who still had a few days left in his term of office, was being blocked from taking any action during the period immediately preceding the inauguration of Joe Biden. The Democrats were in charge, but no one emerged as the leader, including the president-elect.

Finally, on January 20, Joseph C. Biden was inaugurated as the forty-sixth president of the United States. In what was normally a big and important national historic event, it turned out to be a largely television event. There were no protests, and the reports right-wing protestors and Trump supporters were going to disrupt the inauguration tuned out to be not true. The media had misled the country. Doug and his fellow agents spent most of the day in their cubicles at WFO, watching television news and waiting for something to happen. Even after President Biden was safely ensconced in the White House for the night, the agents had to remain at the WFO for several hours. It was another long day before they could go home.

After the inauguration, politics returned to normal, but the District remained in lockdown. The now Democrat-controlled Congress went back to appropriating money for their special interests. Except for signing a number of executive orders, President

Biden disappeared from view. The Executive Branch functioned without anyone really saying who is in charge. The media had little to report. There were no more protests, but the fencing around the Capitol remained in place to protect the members of Congress. The agents of WFO went back to their normal duties.

Chapter 16

Commander Margaret Cassidy was transferred from the DIA to a staff position in the Office of the National Security Advisor to the president. Her experience as a military historian and intelligence officer, coupled with her Mandarin language skills, would be important when it came time for the National Security Advisor to advise President Biden on Chinese security matters and policy.

Margaret's transfer was more in the nature of an assignment as opposed to an appointment. There was nothing political about it. It was not the kind of move which called for a big celebration. Some would even say it was it was not a career-enhancing move for her. Nonetheless, the Gregory's celebrated it with their Aunt Peggy. On the weekend before she reported to the White House, it was party time, which included Bobby and Charley. A good time was had by all.

Changes were being made at the FBI too, but they were not necessarily political. The Bureau agent who was the FBI's liaison to the Joint Intelligence Task Force (JITF) at the CIA was retiring. This is different than the Counter-Intelligence Center (CDC) at the FBI, which focuses on preventing the acquisition of weapons of mass destruction and domestic spying. The Bureau would need to replace the special agent at the CIA. In an unusual request from the CIA, the name of SA Douglas Gregory was floated. The Bureau looked at who might best fill this position and out of the half dozen candidates they considered qualified, none appeared to be any more qualified than SA Gregory.

Once again, Doug was called to come into to SOG for an interview. He had no warning and had no idea what this interview was all about. The people in the HR branch had changed. Doug was no longer dealing with the same people who helped him when he had to work using a cover name. Woody was gone. This time he was directed to the Office of the Executive Assistant Director (EAD) of HR. The interviewer knew SA Gregory had been at WFO for little more than a year and had reviewed his personnel file.

To alleviate any immediate fears that Gregory may have had about being transferred to another city, the interviewer told him, "We need you in another position here in Washington, DC, and I want to offer you a local transfer." It was then explained instead of reporting to WFO, his office would be at the CIA compound in nearby Langley, Virginia.

His job as the FBI representative on a multi-agency JITF would be to coordinate the dissemination the domestic intelligence gathered by the FBI with the other intelligence agencies represented on the IJTF, and to report back to the FBI on any foreign intelligence information the other agencies had, which would be of interest to the Bureau. It all came as a surprise to Doug. Since this was an offer, he asked when the Bureau needed his decision. The position would become available at the end of the month. If Doug was not interested in the position, the Bureau would need time to bring in someone else, likely from out of town. An answer by Monday would be appreciated.

Doug was not sure if this offer of reassignment was a promotion or just a move, but he thought it might be an interesting job. He would miss his work in WFO, but the nice thing was it was a transfer which would not require him and Blair to move or change their lifestyle. It beat the hell out of a transfer to the New York City office. He was inclined to accept the position, but felt he had to discuss it with his wife.

That evening, he thought he would have a little fun with her. At dinner, he asked Blair if he were transferred and he had a choice, where would she like to live? She did not bite on the possibility of an imminent transfer out of the Washington, DC, area. She knew her husband was not on the administrative advancement track in the Bureau, and the FBI did not transfer "Brick Agents" after just one year in a field office unless there was a problem. Doug had not indicated he was having any kind of problem at work. After a few seconds of thought, she said, "How about Florida or Hawaii?" Her answer kind of caught him by surprise. Doug felt a little let down his fun question did not generate the response he thought he would get. He was expecting her to ask if they were being transferred. She then added, "Why did you ask?"

He told her he had been offered what amounts to an intra-office transfer, but they would not be moving. He would be leaving WFO and the Chinese squad and moving to an office position at the CIA headquarters in Langley. He explained his responsibilities of the new position. She replied saying only if she, the boys, and their next child did not have to move, what he did in the Bureau was his call. She was happy with where they were living. So much for his plan to have fun with Blair over the announcement about the job transfer.

On Monday morning, the first thing Doug did when he got to his cubicle at WFO was call over to HR at the SOG and tell them he was interested in accepting the transfer of positions. He was told, since February was a short month and there were only four workdays left until the end of the month, to stay in touch with his office for instructions. After the call to the SOG, he thought he better discuss what was happening with his WFO supervisor. It turns out his supervisor had already had a heads-up the offer had been made to Doug, and WFO was just waiting to hear if he accepted the transfer.

The tentative departure plan was for Doug to contact all his SI contacts and to let them know someone else would be their "handler." All his other cases would be reassigned too. For the rest of this week, he was to spend as much time as possible at the National Security

Branch, being briefed on the responsibilities of his new position. It was a busy week.

Giving up contact with good SI sources was like saying goodbye to a family member. First it was Chen Fang in San Francisco, and now it was Jenny Ling. You spend a lot of time developing them as sources, but they are not people you usually maintain a personal relationship with. It was time for Doug to move on with his professional life.

When Doug was finished each day at WFO, he would spend the rest of the day in the NSB. He was told that while everyone he worked with on the JITF had top secret and the other necessary security clearances, not every agency representative had a need to know about certain matters. It is not a work situation where everyone had access to everything that is going on. While his communication links with the Bureau were secure links, as opposed to internet links which could be hacked, not everything he had access to from the FBI could be shared. Doug's primary function as the FBI representative on the JITF would be to determine what FBI intelligence he had access to could and should be passed on to the other agencies' representatives on the task force.

Under our Constitution and laws, Americans have special rights which foreigners do not have, and the FBI has a responsibility to protect those rights. The sharing of domestic intelligence is a big responsibility. This was the easy part of his new assignment since the

SOG would already have first cut on the propriety of dissemination. The other part of his job was to pass back to the FBI any and all foreign intelligence shared by the JITF, which may be of interest to the FBI because of its domestic jurisdictions. The only information screening he had to do with the foreign intelligence was to evaluate the source and determine if the FBI could make use of it. He did not have to concern himself if any other agency on the JITF acted improperly in releasing their intelligence. It was going to be an interesting job.

On Friday, he was directed to report into the HR security office of the CIA in Langley. Following the instructions given him about how get on the property and check into the facility, he finally made it. The Bureau had given him some of the passes he would need at the CIA, but there were other security measures in the building he would have to learn and use. Eventually he made his way to the JITF work area. There he was introduced the chief of the JITF, John Zhang, the person he knew as Spooky 1 in Monterey. What a surprise.

It turns out it was not a surprise to Zhang that Doug Gregory was joining the JITF. After having been told by Kenneth Yang the student they knew as Robert Allen in Mandarin language school was working in Washington, DC, and having talked to some people at the Bureau about him, Zhang was the one who floated Gregory's name for the FBI vacancy on the JITF. It is a small world—especially in the intelligence community (IC).

Doug was not sure his wife had a need to know about now working with a CIA classmate from language school. Blair had not met anyone from the Mandarin class, but Margaret knew Spooky 1 so he thought best to bring Blair up to speed. John Zhang was probably not his real name anyway.

Like most weekends, Aunt Peggy came by to see "her nephews." They were always glad to see her because she always brought them something. This time, Blair fixed one of her gourmet dinners. After the boys went to bed, Doug and Blair sat down with Margaret to talk about their job changes and everything which had been going on in the nation's capital. A job working in the White House seemed glamorous, so Blair pressed Margaret to tell about her new position.

Margaret started by saying, "First of all, I don't work in the White House. I work in the offices of the NSC, which are in the New Executive Office Building (NEOB) on 17th Street, across the street from the White House. So far I haven't had any real business reason to go over to the West Wing. The White House mess in the West Wing is a great place to eat, so I usually go there for lunch."

Margaret went on to say the national security advisor is a relatively young Ivy Leaguer who has worked in government since college and was an advisor to Hillary Clinton during her 2016 presidential campaign. He has no real-world experience doing anything important but was a loyal Obama–Biden foot soldier. He was a Steele

Dossier Truther during the Russia-Russia Hoax and was involved in trying to frame Lieutenant General Michael Flynn when the general was the national security advisor to President Trump. He has been known to lie about anything and everything. He has little or no credibility among professionals. She asked, "Does it sound like an exciting place to work?"

With that Margaret wanted to change the subject. She wanted to know if Doug was looking forward to his new assignment. He proffered, "I think so."

He went on to explain it will be different than what he has been doing, but he should be able to develop a greater understanding of what is really going on in the world. In his previous position, gathering limited information from sources in a position to know, it was easy to see what the media and often the government was telling the public was not necessarily true and was often intentionally misleading. He added that when you are a special agent in the field, collecting intelligence from sources, you do not necessarily get to see the whole picture. You submit your intel to the Bureau, and there someone else, who has access to other intel on the same subject, gets to analyze it. In his position on the JITF, he will get to see the FBI analysis of the intelligence collected by the Bureau. To the extent there is intelligence collected by other agencies on the JITF that may be of interest to the FBI, he may get to see their analysis too.

He was not sure if Margaret knew he would be working with Spooky 1. He asked her if she remembered John Zhang. That drew a blank stare from her. Doug guessed Spooky 2 had not briefed her. He went on to explain Spooky 1 heads up the JITF, and probably Kenneth Yang had something to do with Greg getting the job.

Chapter 17

Doug reported to his new duty station the following Monday morning. John Zhang and about twenty other people in the room were already at their computers and appeared to be hard at work. Doug had not thought about it, but the JITF functions 24/7. When Doug entered the room, Zhang turned up the room lights, which was apparently a signal to stop what you were doing for a minute while someone made an announcement. John Zhang introduced Doug as the new FBI Rep on the JITF. Then he turned down the overhead lights, and everything appeared to return to normal like magic. Some of the people in the room came over to meet him. Some were obviously in the middle of what they were working on. John Zhang came over to help Doug boot up his terminal. Doug had received training at the SOG in preparation for his assignment, so he knew what he was supposed to do. He started reviewing the FBI analysis submissions since they were last looked at by the JITF/FBI representative. Some were obviously to be forwarded to one of the other agency representatives on the JITF. Some required a quick one-on-one discussion with the rep of one of the other agencies, and some were to be saved for one of the several group meetings the reps would have throughout the day. While he was considering all this, he was getting intel analysis in his terminal "inbox" from the other people in the room.

The first day on the job, Doug became so engrossed in what he was doing, he did not even take a bathroom break. Finally, Zhang came over to him to tell him it was lunch time and suggested he might want to grab something to eat. Doug was a little embarrassed but agreed. Zhang suggested they have lunch together. They adjourned to the CIA cafeteria. While they had lunch, they got caught up the best they could on what each had been doing since Monterey.

Doug told John about a piece of intel he picked up in San Francisco back in late 2018 about a shipment of a virus vaccine from Wuhan which was smuggled into the US just before the outbreak of the COVID-19 virus in January 2019. Doug told John he was just curious if the intel was any good. John said he did not know anything about it because that was before he came to the JITF. John said he would attempt to look it up. Doug went on to explain the reason for his curiosity was that a Chinese student he met in undergraduate school is reputed to be the scientist working at the lab in Wuhan, who developed a vaccine before the outbreak in China.

After lunch, it was back to the computer to go through his in box. Things were beginning to pile up. Those items of intel, which would be of interest to the FBI, were forwarded to the Bureau. The other pieces of intel were catalogued and saved. Nothing goes in the trash. Again, time got away from Doug. All of a sudden, he realized he was going to be late getting home, and he had not called Blair. He used an unclassified telephone line outside of his work area to call home. No one uses cell phones inside the building at the CIA.

By the time Doug got home, the boys were ready for bed. He went through his usual bedtime procedure with them before sitting down with Blair to eat the meal she had saved for him. She knew it must have been a rough day. They did not talk about the intelligence he had reviewed during the day, but he did tell her he did not get out of his chair enough during the day. He was sore from just sitting. He did not say anything to Blair about it, but he briefly reflected on the massage Margaret once gave him, and he wondered if Blair would be as good at it.

The conversation then switched gears and Blair started telling him about the call she received from one of the ladies she had been invited to play golf with last summer. Apparently, with the weather improving, the golfers were making their plans to return to the links. Of course, they wanted to know if they could include Blair. When she told the caller, she was expecting and would not be playing much golf this summer, the caller was disappointed. Blair then said she would like to stay in touch with them and would be glad to help out during any outings they may have. They then agreed to have lunch and to talk about it.

The problem was when to get together. Because of the boys, Blair could not get away for lunch on a weekday. Due to the COVID-19 pandemic, they had not yet engaged anyone to babysit except Aunt Margaret. She is only available on weekends. The invitation led to a discussion with Doug about joining one of the area country clubs, so they would have a place where the boys could play and learn to swim, assuming the pandemic restrictions were lifted. He agreed they needed to look into it.

In the meantime, Blair decided she would invite the ladies golf group to their house for lunch and just see how the boys handled it. When the time came for the gathering, Doug pitched in the evening before to prepare some of the foods. It was a going to be a luncheon to behold. There were six female guests, two from each of three different country clubs. Apparently, they regularly have inter-club tournaments, and these ladies were the movers and shakers from their clubs, at least as far as ladies golf was concerned. Five of them were married to successful husbands and one was a middle-aged widow. The boys ate just before the guests arrived and went down for their naps without a problem. The golf ladies enjoyed their get together and left before Bobby and Charley got up. It was perfect timing, and the guests were impressed both by the food and Blair's management of the luncheon.

The day after the luncheon, one of the ladies called Blair to thank her for hosting the group. Her name was

Bev, and she was married to a Washington, DC, lawyer who had been nominated as an assistant secretary of defense in the Biden administration. She was extremely complimentary about how Blair pulled off the luncheon and said she looked forward to getting to know Blair and her husband.

Doug was settling in well at the JITF. It was more interesting than he thought it would be. There are eighteen US intelligence organizations or agencies in the intelligence community (IC). All are represented on the JITF, but not always by someone from each of the separate intelligence organization. There are a half dozen military intel organizations, which for the most part, work through the DIA rep. The State Department, Treasury, Energy, Drug Enforcement Administration, and the NSA all had someone on duty during normal duty hours, as did the FBI. When there was not a separate agency rep on duty, a CIA duty officer would forward intel traffic. Perhaps the most interesting part of the job was the round table conference to discuss and analyze conflicting intel traffic that came into the JITF.

During the early period of Doug's assignment to the JITF, a lot of intel traffic from the FBI was concerning the protests and riots in the nation's capital. The FBI collected info from local law enforcement and their local criminal and intelligence sources, analyzed it and sent it on the IJTF for distribution. Then the JITF passed it on to the agencies which might need the intel to react. In this case, typically this info would be passed on to the DHS, the DEA, the Department of Energy, and the Army Intelligence Service. State Department, Treasury, and DIA might also be interested since they have a presence in the District.

What was interesting to Doug was that the media was reporting intel about widespread right-wing plans to disrupt post inauguration activities in DC. What the intel showed was there were going to be little or no right-wing protest after the January 6 siege of the Capitol. The principal sources of intel reported by the media were the result of one isolated internet posting, and the media appeared to use the same anonymous sources to prop up each other's stories.

Despite the actual intel, which was given widespread distribution within the government, the powers to be in the government followed the media reports. The FBI director publicly reported the single internet allegation as indicating a potential threat. The speaker of the house, Nancy Pelosi, claimed right-wing protestors were still a major threat to the members of Congress. Fencing around the Capitol, put up after January 6, would have to remain for months, if not permanently.

A week after Blair's golf luncheon, she got an invitation from Bev for her and Doug to come to dinner on Saturday evening. Aunt Peggy said she would be glad to babysit Bobby and Charley. Blair thought this would be a great opportunity to get out and meet some people. The COVID-19 restrictions had made it exceedingly difficult to have any kind of social life outside of the family.

Bev and her husband Dick were very gracious hosts, and it was a pleasant evening for all. It turned out the lawyer Blair had been working with at Google, just before she left the company, was a lawyer from the same law firm in Washington, DC, as Dick. They were well acquainted. It made it even more comfortable politically when they found out Blair had worked as a volunteer at the DNC before the election.

Of course, Doug could not talk about his work, but there was nothing classified about the political happenings in and around the District. While Dick had been nominated for a Democrat appointment to the Department of Defense (DoD), he had not yet been confirmed, and said he was not privy to what was going on in the DoD since Biden was inaugurated. Blair asked about who decided to "lock down" the District and why? Who decided the fencing around the Capitol was necessary, and who was in charge of deciding when it could be taken down? Dick smiled and told her those were all sixty-four-thousand-dollar questions.

Dick proffered he did not know for sure who made the decision to put the fencing up after the protests on January 6. It was clear to him the only people who could have managed a project of that size in such a short period of time would have been the US Army Corps of Engineers. While the Pentagon had to be involved in putting up the fencing, the order to do it had probably come from somewhere else.

The White House and the Executive Branch have little control over what happens in the District itself. About all the WH really controls is the area immediately around the White House itself. The rest of the "city" is divided up into little fiefdoms. There is the mayor and city council which control nongovernment events. There is the Military District of Washington, which is largely ceremonial, but controls the military facilities in the District. Then there are two other co-equal branches of government, the Judicial and the Congress, which control their facilities. In the case of the Capitol and the area surrounding it, the Speaker of the House is in charge, but little or nothing happens in or around the Capitol unless it is approved and requested by the Capitol architect. No one has claimed responsibility for making the decision to put up the fencing. Probably because it serves no public purpose, except to exercise *control* and project *power*.

The discussion then went back to the issue of who was responsible for determining when the fencing should be taken down and when is that likely to happen. The answer was kind of the same but was a little more complicated because there are still some seven thousand Army National Guard (ARNG) troops in the District. The fence will not likely be taken down until the National Guard leaves. Nancy Pelosi does not control when the ARNG will leave. The new Secretary of Defense has suggested he is considering withdrawing the ARNG troops, but it is not clear he has the authority. These forces have not been federalized and still belong to the governors of the states from which they came. Then there is the mayor who wants to be put in control of the District of Columbia's National Guard. No one seems to know who is in charge of this decision. In the meantime, everything remains status quo. The conclusion of the dinner group that evening was if it is about power, Nancy Pelosi was in "the cat bird seat." In Washington, DC, *power* and *control* are everything.

As Blair got to know more of the ladies from the golf group, it was apparent their husbands and circle of political friends kept the girls well informed about the gossip within what had become known during the Trump administration as "The Swamp." Basically, it is group of politicians and "want to be" people who perennially operate inside Washington political circles, no matter who appears to be in charge. While Blair would probably never become a member of the Swamp, she was developing contacts with people who were. One of them could even be the next Perle Mesta, American socialite and diplomat who entertained lavishly.

⟶⟶⟶ Chapter 18 ⟵⟵⟵

During the first one hundred days of the Biden administration, Washington, DC, continued in total lockdown, ostensibly because of continued concern over the spread of the COVID-19 virus. The president and his staff continued to wear face masks and demand everyone else wear one too. This continued to instill fear in some of the American public and allowed the WH to exercise more *control* of government events. The president seldom appeared in public, except to be shown signing over more than thirty executive orders, directing actions to be taken by the Executive Branch.

While most of the executive orders dealt with simply reversing policies of the previous administration, the order to immediately discontinue the building of the wall between Mexico and the United States had a major impact on immigration events. The wall, which had been paid for in full, would remain unfinished. Biden's orders to the US Immigration and Customs Enforcement (ICE) agency to immediately stop deporting illegal aliens, and for the other border authorities to allow all minors seventeen years of age and under to enter the country, caused an immediate huge influx of immigrants coming through Mexico.

Many families traveling together were also admitted and released into the US without restrictions. Most were not tested for the COVID-19 virus. Even those who were tested and found to be positive for the virus were released into the community without being treated. While all this was going on, the media was denied access to information about the numbers of people and what facilities had been set up to deal with the influx. The WH claimed the situation was under control, but opposition political figures who were able to gain access to the border facilities were reporting it was a crisis in the making.

In the midst of the crisis, the Democrat-controlled House of Representative and Senate passed a 1.9 trillion spending bill, which they referred to as a COVID Relief Bill. Less than seven percent of the money appropriated in this bill was actually for COVID virus relief. The rest was for Democrat spending on other things over the next ten years. It was all about building power and maintaining control of the government spending for years to come. President Biden signed the spending bill.

While President Biden kept saying he was being transparent there were little or no explanations about what was really going on in the government. The president had not scheduled the traditional State of the Union address and had only held one press conference. Even the one "presser" was one in which Biden used cue cards to answer questions from reporters who had been handpicked to ask their questions. The WH was in control of the press conferences and communications, but it was not a problem for the media because they were in total support of Biden and the Democrats.

The COVID-19 debacle seemed not to have much direct effect on the Gregory family. The fact the CDC and the Biden administration were keeping COVID good news from the public seemed to be causing a lot of consternation around the country. This had been going on for over a year, and President Trump's vaccine program was continuing well under the new WH. The question was how much longer would the government try to control events and public actions caused by the virus?

In some states, students were attending school, and in many other states they were attending classes online. However, in some communities, there had been no schooling since right after the pandemic began. Most notable of these were Chicago and Los Angeles, where the teacher's unions were opposing the reopening of schools until teachers could get the vaccine. The education system of the country was a mess, but the administration claimed they had it under control. In reality, the teacher's unions, instead of parents, were in control of student learning.

The problem in the US was politics and control had taken over from the principles of freedom and law and order Americans value so much. Small businesses were failing, worship was limited for some, personal movement was sometimes restricted, and the mental health of the people of the nation was being threatened.

The people of the country were losing control of their freedom and lives.

Blair was a survivor, so pandemic restriction had little effect on her and the boys. They really did not have to go out that often. For Doug, it was a little more inconvenient, but because he worked in Virginia rather than in the District, it was somewhat easier to deal with. The person who had the biggest challenge was Margaret, since she worked in what is considered was part of the WH compound. She had to wear a mask 24/7 when she had to go into the District. She regained her personal freedom only when she got home or went to the Gregory house on weekends.

In the JITF, there was still a lot of traffic about the spread and mutations of the virus in Europe and other parts of the world, but none of it was consistent. Just like the reporting in the US, the number of new cases and deaths around the world from the virus depended on who was reporting the information. WHO was strangely silent on the number of new virus cases. If they overreported the numbers, it made their friend China look bad. If they underreported the numbers, it would make it appear the virus crisis was ending. You cannot maintain control without a crisis, and those in control "never let a crisis go to waste."

➤➤ Chapter 19 ◄◄◄

Since President Biden announced that immigrants crossing the border from Mexico would no longer be turned away, the intel traffic from multiple sources had been humming. FBI agents assigned to work in Mexico (known as legal attachés, or Legats) have been developing some of the most crucial information about the numbers of immigrants and who they are. Since the agents are on the ground in Mexico and work with the Mexican Federales, the intel is exceptionally good but not always perfect. This information is immediately passed by the JITF to DHS, DEA, and a number of other intelligence agencies whose departments have responsibility to react to what is happening.

In one month, the US Border Patrol stopped fourteen people trying to enter the US from Mexico who were not Central Americans. They were from Iran, China, India, Haiti, several African nations, and other countries. Since the Border Patrol is unable to stop all the people crossing the border, there is no telling how many of these non-Central Americans successfully entered the US without being identified. It is estimated that for every single illegal immigrant stopped at the border, two others enter without being stopped. Some of the fourteen who were caught were identified as spies or terrorists. It is logical to assume some of those who entered and were not caught at the border were also spies or terrorist. These unknown immigrants are the ones the FBI will be looking to find and identify.

Just reviewing of this intel traffic was keeping Doug busy. The table conferences in the JITF to resolve conflicting intel were many. What was clear was a policy decision by the new president had created mass migration through Mexico, and the US government was not prepared to handle it. The Mexican government was also in crisis because of this change in policy. Besides being told to "stand-down" on their efforts to prevent the migration, Mexico also had to deal with the drug cartels who were making millions of dollars trafficking immigrants. The cartels were charging anywhere from $2,500.00 to get a Central American into the US to $25,000.00 for an Iranian, a Chinese person, or someone from India.

At least one report from the DEA referred to cartel money from the trafficking being paid to Democrat politicians supporting the migration and open-border policies. The source indicated this financial support was actually negotiated before the president's policy was announced. CIA analysts wanted to dismiss the intelligence because it was not specific, but it was disseminated by the JITF with a CIA disclaimer attached as to its credibility. What was clear is the cartels were in control of the southern border of the United States and smuggling immigrants across it.

During a quiet moment in the JITF, John Zhang took Doug aside and told him he had gone back and looked at the intelligence on Daniel Chen and the virus vaccine supposedly produced in Wuhan before the pandemic. He confirmed reports that Dr. Daniel Chen and a team of scientists at the lab in Wuhan were believed to have been working on anti-viral technology. Several of the international pharmaceutical companies were also involved in this research in Wuhan. There were a few unconfirmed reports of their success, but there are no medical or science journal reports confirming they had developed an effective vaccine. There were also multiple intel reports of a vaccine being smuggled into the United States in November and December 2018.

Zhang reminded Doug all this information on Wuhan and the virus was highly classified and not for distribution. The only reason Zhang was telling him about the intelligence was because Doug had two connections to the matter. If it ever came out the Chinese intentionally released the COVID virus on the world intentionally to gain control, it could be grounds for declaring war on China.

Blair could tell the boys were getting restless. They had to spend too much time indoors this past winter.

She and Doug had to get them out more. The weekend with Aunt Peggy will provide a good opportunity if the weather cooperates. When Saturday came, they were ready to go, and the five of them headed to a nearby park. Blair packed a picnic lunch. This would be their first outing of the season.

While they played in the park, Doug asked Margaret how it was going. She said it was very interesting being where the action was but frustrating working with people who are amateurs and think they are experts. Getting the national security advisor ready for his trip to Alaska to meet with the Chinese was a challenge. Her part was to bring him up to date on Chinese naval power, their forays in the South China Sea, and the impact of the dispute over Sansha City. Others on the staff briefed him on other issues. He was probably given too much information. She was not sure he absorbed much of it.

After a fun picnic, they went back to the house so the boys could take a nap. Although the boys were only two and a half years old, they were both very active. They needed the rest. Once they were down, Doug pulled the cork on a bottle of red wine. Blair stuck with the sparkling water. Blair then offered a toast to the next member of our family, a daughter who will be named "Reed." She explained she had been to the doctor on Friday and that she is far enough along in the pregnancy they could determine she was carrying a girl. Doug was elated, and Aunt Peggy was excited.

Doug and Blair had already decided on Anne as a middle name, if it was a girl. Her name would be Reed Anne Gregory. Being a very clever person, Margaret immediately picked up on her initials being RAG. She dubbed her new niece Raggedy Anne. Her first gift from Aunt Peggy would undoubtedly be a Raggedy Ann doll.

Later in the afternoon, when the boys woke up, Blair and Aunt Peggy got them ready for the rest of the day. In between activities, entertaining the twins, the conversation of the adults was about where the country was going. The three of them agreed the Biden administration had done a one-hundred-eighty-degree turn from the policies of the Trump administration. Were there that many people in the country who did not like the successes of the last four years? Not really. The consensus was while there may have been a lot of voters who disliked Trump personally, but that was not the reason for his defeat. The Democrats took control of the election process, which resulted in them taking control of the Executive Branch and the Congress. This put them in a position to take permanent control of the future of the country.

After the weekend, it was back to work for all. Zhang had duties out of the building, so he asked Doug to fill in for him as the JITF duty officer, which was not a problem for Doug. Just before lunch, a duty officer from another section of the CIA came into the JITF looking for John. Doug explained that John had gone down to "The Farm" for the day to teach a class.

Doug asked if he could help him. Not realizing Doug was the FBI representative in the JITF and not a CIA employee, the visitor shared info from a CIA "Eyes Only" file, indicating there was a mole in the White House. The question the visitor had was whether this intel had been distributed and to whom? Doug knew he had not previously seen the information, and he could not find on his computer terminal where the previous FBI representative on the JITF had sent it to the Bureau. Doug could not answer the question, so he said he would pass the matter to John on his return the next day. John would have to take care of it tomorrow.

Over lunch, Doug had chance to think about the morning visit. What he had learned from the CIA officer was extremely sensitive intelligence, which required limited dissemination so that it would not be compromised. He concluded since FBI Counter-Intel was responsible for "spy catching" inside the country, it should have the information. After lunch, he decided to send the report to the Bureau. If it had previously been sent to the Bureau, no harm done.

Later in the day, Doug received a telephone call from the Bureau asking him to come into the FBI headquarters, National Security Branch, the next morning. They want to discuss the intel report he had sent earlier in the day. Before leaving the JITF for the day, he sent a message to John telling him about the question which had come up earlier in the day and asking him to get with the CIA duty officer who had visited the IJTF.

It was not a matter for discussion at home that evening. All he told Blair was he had to go into the Bureau in the morning and expected to be back in his office in Langley after lunch. The next morning when he arrived at the SOG, he was directed to the Office of the Executive Assistant Director (EAD) of the National Security Branch.

The EAD got straight to the point. He said, "We have a problem. The intel you sent us yesterday is information which we should have had earlier, but it appears the CIA has been withholding it. Do they know you disseminated to us yesterday?"

Doug told the EAD he had not yet had a discussion with the CIA officer in the JITF.

The EAD added, "Unless he asks you, leave it be. We will put a clamp on the source of the intel as long as we can. Let us know if you are challenged about sending it to us. The worst-case scenario is they kick you out of the JITF, and we have to find another place for you."

Doug told the EAD he realizes the FBI will begin an investigation to determine if there is a mole somewhere in the WH, and that this would include people who work for the national security advisor. He wanted to the Bureau to know he had a personal and family-like relationship with a Naval officer he met in language school several years ago and who works in the WH. The

AD thanked him for that additional information and sent Doug on his way.

Back at Langley, he settled into his duties as normal. Nothing was said about Doug being gone in the morning. There was nothing unusual about agency reps being called into their home office for something. Doug asked John he if was able to get back with the duty officer about the CIA intel report question. John said he had. That was the end of their discussion on the matter.

The discussion Doug had with the EAD put him to thinking about the mole in the WH probably being someone works in the Office of the National Security Advisor. This would be the most logical place to put a spy. He thought to himself, *For God's sake, don't let it be Margaret Cassidy.*

➤➤ Chapter 20 ➤➤

If Washington, DC, was a ship, it would sink. There are so many leaks in it, there is no way it could stay afloat. Such is the case with the information about the FBI investigating the possibility of a mole working in the White House.

It was only a couple of weeks after SA Douglas Gregory had forwarded the CIA information about a mole to the Bureau, it became apparent there was a high-level leak at the Bureau. For Doug, it all came to light when John Zang took him aside and told him about the problem. The CIA had learned the FBI had an active investigation going on about a possible mole, and the predicate for the investigation was a CIA report. The people at the CIA were distressed because they had not yet disseminated the information. It was still highly classified and was still "Eyes Only" at the Agency.

The CIA was conducting their own internal investigation to see if there was a leak at The Company. Over the weekend they checked all the terminals in the IJTF and found the report Doug sent to the Bureau the day John was out of pocket. John warned Doug he might be called to go "Upstairs" at the CIA to explain this unauthorized release of classified information, and to be prepared to defend his actions. Doug was taken back about John referring to the release as being "unauthorized" and knew he better try to get some help. This could be a serious matter.

Doug recalled the conversation he had with the EAD of the National Security Branch the day after he sent the CIA information to the Bureau. He thought he would start there. Doug signed out of the IJTF for the day and headed for the J. Edgar Hoover Building. On the way, he got on his cell phone and called ahead for an appointment. He asked for an emergency meeting with the EAD. When he got to the SOG, he went straight to the EAD's office. On his arrival, he had to wait a few minutes. The EAD was on an important telephone call.

The EAD said, "I just got off the phone with lawyers from the CIA. They are livid about the unauthorized dissemination of the information about there being a mole in the White House. I tried to tell them since the FBI has primary jurisdiction in this matter. I was more concerned with the CIA sitting on the information and it not being disseminated earlier. They just ignored my concerns. It looks like we are in a 'Mexican Stand-Off' with them."

Doug wanted to know where he stood in all of this. The EAD told him he had a technical problem and may want to get legal counsel. The EAD explained the Bureau's problem and Doug's problem were different. It is the adage about there being two parts to the rule on dissemination of classified information: one being you only make dissemination to people who have the required level of clearance. The other being you only disseminate to people who "have the need to know." Unfortunately, sometimes it is the people or organization who are in possession of the information who think only they know who gets to see the information. There was no problem with the proper level of security being observed here, but the CIA claims they had sole control of the information until they decided who had the need to know, and Doug should not have sent that information to the FBI. Prior to the CIA making that determination, any dissemination was technically unauthorized.

The EAD went on to tell Doug the FBI lawyers could advise on what the FBI should do, but they could not represent Doug or advise him on what he should do. There will undoubtedly be some inquiry by the lawyers in the Justice Department concerning Doug's actions, but whether the CIA "wants to fall on their sword" about keeping the information from the FBI is another issue.

Doug was told to go back to work in the IJTF until either the CIA told him he was persona non grata or the Bureau transferred him. Since he had signed out for the day when he left Langley, he decided to go home and tell Blair about his adventure. He did not discuss the intelligence about there being a mole in the WH, only that he had communicated something to the FBI which the CIA was still trying to keep under wraps.

Blair assured Doug they could handle whatever was required financially. Together they went to work on finding a good attorney to represent Doug. The first call was to the Law Enforcement Legal Defense Fund, which was established during Watergate in to help special agents and police officers who were maliciously charged. He was trying to get the names of attorneys in the Washington, DC, area who have a good reputation for handling these kinds of cases. Doug also called Richard, the lawyer who was waiting confirmation of an appointment to a position in the DoD. Sorting through the lists given them, and with a little online research, Doug and Blair came up with a couple of names.

Since this problem was likely to move fast, Doug placed a call to a female attorney who was well known in the District Bar and had been on television during the Trump administration in defense of the Russia-Russia Hoax and several people in the administration. Doug introduced himself and gave the receptionist a brief explanation of why he was calling. She transferred him to a paralegal who took more information from Doug. The paralegal told him they would get back to him within twenty-four hours, but in the meantime not to discuss the case with anyone else. Doug knew this was good advice.

The following morning, he went to work as usual. John Zhang did not say anything until mid-morning, when he told Doug the CIA security people wanted to talk to him about the breach. Since John was in effect his supervisor in the IJTF, Doug told John to pass the word back to them he was represented by an attorney and had been told not to speak to anyone about the matter. John understood where Doug was coming from and said he would take care of it.

Doug decided to leave the grounds at Langley at lunch time so he could check for messages on his cell phone. The attorney had called and left a call back message. Doug picked up some fast food, found a shady spot in a nearby park, and called the attorney. She said she would like to talk more to him about the case and was available to represent him if they agreed. Doug asked when she was available. She could see him in her office at 5 o'clock. Not a good time of day for traffic in the District, but he was anxious to meet with her. Doug went back to the IJTF for a while and then left early to drive to the attorney's office. He called Blair to bring her up to date on what was happening and told her to just put his dinner in the refrigerator. He would eat when he got home. She was glad he was meeting with the attorney.

The conference was attended by Doug, the attorney, and her paralegal. It lasted almost two hours. Before leaving, Doug had agreed to her representing him and the fee. This was not going to be cheap. She told him just refer everyone who wants to talk to him about the matter to her office, including the people at the FBI. She had some doubts about the CIA wanting to pursue the matter, but it was a politically sensitive subject, and sometimes matters like this get off track. She would try to resolve it just as quickly as possible.

The attorney told Doug, the IJTF at the CIA was an "off the books" operation, meaning it was not an overt part of the intelligence community (IC). It was set up by the CIA as a way of attempting to avoid the dissemination minimization requirements imposed on the IC while sharing intelligence. The CIA is not likely to make too big a deal of this matter, since it could expose the existence of a "black operation."

The boys were already in bed when their dad got home, so he went into their bedroom and kissed each one goodnight. Then he sat down with Blair to eat his warmed-up dinner and go over the events of the day. He had no idea of what tomorrow would bring.

The next day when he got to Langley and tried to enter the building, his pass did not work. He apparently had been locked out. Just to make sure it was not just a technical problem he checked with security. They confirmed his entry pass had been revoked. He thought about it for a moment and then left the building. He would let his attorney and the FBI worry about it.

Once out the area of the CIA, he called his attorney to let her know what happened and left a report with the paralegal. Then he put in a call to the Bureau to see what they wanted him to do. He wound up talking to the associate executive assistant director who told him to "sit tight" until they got back to him. He took it to mean do not come in to the SOG until someone decided something. Doug then decided he could sit tight at home as easily as anywhere else. Blair was surprised but glad he came home. She fixed him a light lunch.

After lunch, he received a telephone call from the assistant director of the Human Resources Branch informing him he had an appointment at nine o'clock tomorrow morning with the EAD of Human Resources. Doug told Blair he was "grounded" for the rest of the day, and if she had some errands she wanted to run, he would look after the boys. She thought that was nice and decided not to waste the opportunity.

The next morning, he was at the SOG and in the waiting area of the Human Resources EAD, a few minutes before the appointed time. A couple of minutes later, he was invited into the conference room adjoining the EAD's Office. There he was joined by a couple of other Bureau officials, including the AD of the Directorate of Intelligence. For some reason, there was no one from the criminal branch.

The EAD for HR started the meeting off by announcing they were not there to discuss what happened with the CIA. At this time, it was an interagency problem, and the Bureau had no reason to fault SA Gregory. The purpose of this meeting was to discuss options for reassigning Gregory. The reason SA Gregory was there was because this was not a routine transfer or reassignment meeting, and the panel might have questions of him. One of the people from HR briefed the group on SA Gregory's Bureau history.

"SA Douglas Gregory has had some unusual assignments and experiences in the six years he has been an agent. He was sent to Mandarin language school, worked in the San Francisco Division using a cover name, worked at WFO, and was involved in a successful sting operation against Chinese intelligence. His most recent assignment was to the IJTF at Langley. The question is what we should do about another assignment. The problem we have is, given the unresolved dispute with the CIA, the Bureau cannot not transfer SA Gregory out of the Washington, DC, area until the CIA issue is resolved. Questions?"

There were a few questions about the problem with the CIA. Doug was given the opportunity to tell the panel he was represented by counsel and had been advised not to discuss the problem with anyone. The Intel AD added he saw it as a CIA communication issue and not an FBI problem. There is no reason to consider Gregory's part in the CIA debacle a problem for him. There were no questions about Gregory's record.

The remainder of the conference dealt with what positions were available in the Washington, DC, area which would be appropriate for an agent of his experience and service. Whatever they did, it must not give the appearance of a demotion or his being punished. A job as a supervisor in WFO would be appropriate, but currently no vacancies existed. Assignment to the Northern Virginia Resident Agency might work but would not necessarily take advantage of his experience.

One member of the panel suggested since there was so much new activity concerning illegal immigration through Mexico, the International Operations Division might be able to use another agent working intelligence received from the Legats in Mexico. Other possibilities were floated. When the meeting adjourned, Doug was asked to stay available in the afternoon.

Since Doug had not been on the firing range recently and was about due for requalification, he thought it might be a good way to spend the afternoon. The range facilities in the J. Edgard Hoover Building are superb but always busy. After lunch, he spent a couple of hours on the range. Before leaving the building, he went back to HR just to make sure he was no longer needed for the rest of the day. The HR person told him it looked like they had found him a job in the International Ops Division, which is part of the Criminal, Cyber, Response and Services branch, but they would not know until the next morning. Doug was told to return in the morning for developments. It was near the end of the workday anyway, so Doug headed home to tell Blair about his day.

On Friday, he returned to the SOG and the HR Division to see if a decision had been made on his next assignment. They told him the Criminal Branch folks had decided to let him work in the International Ops Division. A lot of immigration intelligence was coming out of Mexico at the present time through the Legats. Because of the special relationship the United States has with Mexico, the Legats operate as law enforcement officials in Mexico and not as intelligence operatives. The FBI considers information received from the Legats as domestic criminal intelligence, and not as foreign intelligence, since it has to do with criminal activities affecting the US. Doug might be tasked to help with the management of the intelligence out of Mexico, or he may be asked to coordinate Legat work in one of the other sixty-two FBI Legal Attaché offices around the world.

Doug was then invited to tour the Legat section work area and to meet the people he would be working with. He spent several hours getting oriented and "learning the ropes." It seemed like it was going to be a good work situation. Since Friday afternoon was probably not a good time to start a new job, he was told to come back the following Monday morning, ready to go. Doug was ready for the weekend.

As usual, Margaret was at the Gregory's on Saturday. She had no inkling Doug had been terminated in the IJTF. Doug just played it low key and told her he had a new assignment at the FBI, and what it was. She thought it was a little unusual for even the FBI to move someone for no reason at all, from one assignment to another after such a short period of time, but she left it alone. If Doug wanted her to know why he would tell her. There was no discussion about the FBI looking for a "sleeper agent" in the WH either. It was just a fun weekend for Aunt Peggy, the boys, Blair, and Doug.

↠ Chapter 21 ↞

Doug's initial assignment in the Legat section was to review reports coming in from the legal attachés in Mexico. Many of the reports contained information on drug cartel operations. This included the movement of drugs from Central America through Mexico and then across the border into the United States. These reports also included a lot of information about the cartels' human trafficking of illegal immigrants into the US. Both are huge money makers for them. Recently the reports have also included a lot of information about who the people crossing into Mexico from Guatemala are.

The border between Mexico and Guatemala is 400 miles long, and it is only partially fenced. Mexico has the same problems on their southern border the US has on its border with Mexico. While many of the immigrants cross the border at checkpoints, it is believed many criminals, terrorists, and non-Central Americans cross into Mexico in rural areas without being checked. Guatemala border crossing data is collected by Legats mostly from Mexican authorities. Some Legats have joined the immigrant groups as they travel through Mexico toward the US border and are able to identify people who are not Central Americans or who may be MS-13 gang members.

Of significant interest to the FBI is the information they get from the Legats about cartel human trafficking activity. It begins in the Northern Triangle countries of Guatemala, Honduras, and El Salvador, where the cartels actively recruit immigrants to come to the US and extract large sums of money to make the trip. Immigrants are given color-coded plastic wristbands to wear during the trip. The color depends on how much money is paid to the cartels. The wristband serves not only as protection passport through the areas of Mexico control by the cartels, but also indicates to the cartel people at the border how the immigrants are to be smuggled into the US. Some will be left at a border checkpoint to be processed, some will cross the Rio Grande River by raft, and some will be walked into the US through the desert. Those who cannot afford to pay will have to serve as "mules" to carry drugs across the border or serve as prostitutes. This has recently become a cash cow for the cartels.

Doug was almost stunned to see not only how much information there was in these reports about the numbers of immigrants who were enroute to the US, but also about the make-up of the people. When verified, the information is passed for use by the FBI branches and other divisions. It is also sent to the Department of Homeland Security, the Border Patrol, the Immigration & Customs Enforcement (ICE), and other departments and local law enforcement agencies responsible for the care of the immigrants when they were admitted into this country. Nobody at the border should be surprised by the numbers or who the immigrants are. However, by the time they reach the border, only about one-third of the immigrants are actually processed, mostly males traveling alone. The presumption is the rest of the illegal immigrants cross the border into the United States without being processed.

The handling of immigrants under the previous administration was considered inhumane because immigrants were either forced to remain in Mexico while asylum claims were heard, or they were immediately repatriated to their home country. Because of a policy change by the Biden administration, very few immigrants are now turned away at the border. Lack of planning for this change in policy has resulted in a crisis. Immigrants are being housed in substandard facilities or being released into the general population of the US without any kind of support.

The section Doug was assigned to is also responsible for coordinating investigative requests sent to the Legats around the world. These are normally generated in an FBI field offices. They have to do with a criminal matter being conducted here in the US.

Doug found the work very interesting. It certainly gave him insight into the crisis at the Mexican border, which seemed to be ignored by the administration. It was kind of like the situation in the District. No one on the US side seemed to be in control at the border. The vice president had been designated by the president as the person to manage the "non-crisis" at the border, but she was nowhere to be found. While a couple of Department secretaries had visited the border, the VP was "Absent Without Leave (AWOL)." Control and power on both sides of the border between Mexico and the United States belonged to the cartels.

Other than identification of the source of the intelligence, little of what Doug dealt with was considered classified information. The news of the days on television was fair game for discussion at home. Blair enjoyed being able to discuss with Doug some of the fallout from the stuff he was working on.

A month or so into his current assignment, Doug received a call from his attorney regarding the status of the problem with the CIA complaint. She advised the CIA offered to resolve their complaint against him if he would agree to a disciplinary reprimand for the improper dissemination of classified information. Since this would affect his ability to keep a top-secret security clearance, and therefore his employment as an FBI agent, she rejected their offer. Instead, she suggested they proceed with a formal complaint in which case she would begin taking the depositions of CIA officials. She would then disclose the CIA was improperly withholding information from the FBI, which was critical to the security of the nation. The process might also identify the CIA's source of the information and ruin their chances of ever identifying the mole. After due consideration, the CIA lawyers advised they would not pursue the matter further and would notify the deputy director of the FBI the matter had been satisfactorily resolved. As far as her representation of Doug was concerned, it was over. He should be notified of this by the Bureau in due course.

Doug was enjoying his assignment and thought he would just sit tight until the Bureau reached out to him about what was next. It was cause for a celebration at home with Blair, but not something they could discuss with Aunt Peggy. There was still the issue of the allegation of a mole in the WH and a leak somewhere in the FBI. After what he had been through, all Doug wanted was to stay away from both issues as long as he could. They had already cost him a lot of money and almost cost him his job.

Doug and Blair discussed what might happen next. He was preparing her for the likelihood of a transfer outside the Washington, DC, area. Did they want to move again? What about the child she was expecting? He could take the Washington, DC, and Virginia Bar exams and practice law without their having to move. Did she want to go back to Florida?

It must have taken a while for the CIA to react to the settlement agreement. It was a couple of more months before the FBI notified Doug he was no longer under assignment restrictions. It all began when Doug was invited to meet with the deputy director who oversees the three investigative branches, and the EAD of the HR branch. It was a very congenial meeting. Both were familiar with what Doug had been through in his FBI career, and with his performance record. This meeting was almost like a mid-career consultation to see what Doug wanted to do. Perhaps they were concerned about losing him after the CIA debacle. They assured him he was in good stead with the Bureau, and they offered him several options to consider. Some were months away from being available, but he was welcome to continue his current temporary assignment until a selected assignment came available.

Blair was pleased with the news about Doug's meeting concerning his future in the FBI, if that is what he wanted to do. At least, it meant for the immediate future they could plan on staying in Virginia until Reed Anne was born. However, the options for the future meant they would be moving on. There are only so many FBI positions in the Washington, DC, area, and Doug had already worked in more than most do in their career.

The decision Doug was now being required to make was whether or not he wanted to move into the management track or continue to be a brick agent. The latter generally can stay in a field office for years or eventually select an office of preference to retire from. Agents who opt for advancement can expect to be moved several times. He was still twenty-plus years away from retirement if he stayed in the Bureau. He was also at an age where, in the future career, changes would become more difficult. The only decision Doug made immediately was to study for and take the District and Virginia Bar Exams.

Some of the possibilities Doug brought home included a transfer to New York City to work United Nations and Chinese intel issues. A transfer to New York would not be particularly career enhancing. There was also a possible assignment in the fall to an intel supervisor's job in WFO. An assignment as a field office supervisor could lead to selection for further advancement. An assignment later this year to a Legat position in Singapore or Manila was also a possibility. Jobs as a Legat are almost a career field unto themselves. A move from investigative work to the Administrative branch of the Bureau was another option. All options were on the table for him. Doug and Blair decided to wait until they saw what the FBI offered Doug.

➤➤ Chapter 22 ◄◄◄

When the call came, it was from the Office of the Deputy Director. Doug was quite surprised by it since he thought his next assignment was going to be his to make in consultation with the HR people. The deputy director told Doug, while reviewing the lack of disclosure problem they were having with the CIA, it brought Doug to mind as a person they could use to help with the WH investigation. The FBI has a very "close hold" on the investigation, looking for the mole, and there are very few people at either the SOG or WFO who are even aware of it—and the fewer the better. While the deputy director did not need or want Doug to be directly involved in the investigation, the investigators could use someone inside the WH who could spot and report activity, which might help them identify the mole.

The FBI normally keeps two special agents assigned to work in the WH. Their work is primarily processing security clearance requests for WH staff and department appointments. They also handle liaison matters, as needed. Right now the agents in the WH are overwhelmed because of large number of clearance requests from a new administration. This presents an opportunity for the FBI to put another agent in the WH, and at the same time help the investigators looking for the mole. The agents who are already in the WH are not aware of the investigation and are not to be told. Since Doug already knew about the investigation, he would be the perfect person to act as the investigators' "eyes and ears" inside the WH. At this point, there was no telling how long this assignment would last, but it could be long term, at least until the FBI identifies the mole. The deputy director told Doug to plan on starting there on Monday.

Chapter 23

The FBI agents assigned to the White House are not part of the White House staff. They occupy office space in the bowels of the Old Executive Office Building (OEOB) and generally have little reason to be in the West Wing. They are there to process the security clearances requested by the WH and seldom have any need to talk with WH staff members. This was going to be a problem for SA Gregory if he was to be the eyes and ears inside the White House for the agents trying to identify the mole. He would need to be creative in order to develop sources on the WH staff, while at the same time keeping the other two FBI agents assigned there from knowing the real purpose of his assignment.

Gregory's first day on the job at the WH was unremarkable. He stuck close to the FBI's office in the OEOB. It was important at the outset he was careful to make sure the other agents did not consider him as their trainee and load him up with files to be processed. All they knew is Gregory was not permanently assigned to them. It was up to him to walk the tight rope between his undercover assignment and his apparent job. At lunch time, he went over to the White House mess in the West Wing to check it out. He had previously made arrangements with Margaret Cassidy not to go there when he would be. Gregory did not want anyone knowing he knew anyone who worked in the WH.

A couple of days into his new assignment, he told the other agents one of his assigned jobs was to review the security clearance files of WH staffers who had already been granted clearances. His review was to make sure nothing had been missed by either the brick agents doing the background checks or the Bureau's processing of the clearances. The real purpose of conducting the file reviews was so he could meet with and interview the staffers in the West Wing and to get to know them personally. This would then open the door for him to have reasons to talk to other staffers. He needed to identify, if he could, who knew what and to see if there was anyone on the staff who might be the mole or who might lead him to that person.

After reviewing a number of security files, he found a couple with minor discrepancies. He thought by taking those first, it would appear his inquiries of the staff were routine. That way no one else would be upset if they were also interviewed. Since the FBI facilities in the OEOB were more like a file room rather than a conference room, he always made sure he could conduct his staff interviews in the West Wing. During these interviews, sometimes it was what he learned from the discussion with the staffer was more important than what was in the staffer's file. As he worked his way through the interviews, he would frequently see the people he interviewed in the WH mess and he often sat with them during lunch.

There were WH staffers who worked in the OEOB and the New Executive Office Building on 17th Street, across from the White House. These people were not to be ignored, including Margaret Cassidy. Once he interviewed Commander Cassidy, he would occasionally have lunch with her in the West Wing. Within just a few weeks, SA Doug Gregory seemed to be known and accepted by most of the staff. No one seemed to mind his being in the West Wing on a regular basis. Everyone was too busy with their work to care about Doug Gregory being there.

The West Wing could be a beehive of activity on weekends, especially if there was a national crisis brewing. Doug stayed away on weekends since it would not be a good time to pull someone aside for a security review, and he might be considered out of place. Occasionally he did go to OEOB on weekends to help with the regular duties of the office, if there was a backlog of security files to process. Being at home on weekends was a perk of the assignment. If the West Wing was quiet, Margaret Cassidy would be off too. This was good time for Aunt Peggy to see the twin boys and to visit with the Gregory family.

On one occasion, when she was visiting Doug and Blair, she got him aside and asked, "Why are you working in the White House? That's not a job for a seasoned agent. Are you in trouble, or is this another one of those 'I shouldn't ask' assignments?"

Doug responded, "No I am not in trouble, and I would appreciate you're not asking about why I am there. Again, you need to pretend like you don't know me, except as the agent who interviewed you to go over your security clearance information. If we meet in the White House mess, no discussion about our family or past relationship. If you have something to tell me about what is going on in the West Wing, save it for the weekend, or if it is urgent, call me on my cell." Margaret knew Doug well enough to suspect he had been placed in the White House for something other than a routine assignment. She would play the game with him.

Chapter 24

B lair was in all her glory. She was about six months pregnant, and everyone was looking forward to the birth of Reed Anne "Raggedy Ann" Gregory. Blair was probably more anxious than the others. It was getting a little harder to manage the boys, and the COVID-19 restrictions still made it difficult to find help. Evening and weekends were a blessing since she had a husband who was very helpful. Besides being able to care for the boys in the evening, he was a good cook, almost as good as Blair.

A couple of weeks into his project of conducting security re-interviews with the WH staffers, he received a call from Katherine Smith, who identified herself as a special agent of the FBI. She told Doug she wanted to discuss his latest Bureau assignment and asked to meet him. He had been expecting this call. They arranged to meet away from the White House and away from the FBI offices. On his way home, he met SA Smith at a convenience store and then rode with her to a nearby apartment in Virginia. The apartment had been rented by the special team investigating the mole in the White House. The apartment served as their office. There was only one other special agent in the apartment when they arrived. They told Doug they were part of a larger team of people brought in from several field offices to conduct the investigation. Other than the deputy director and the team members, Doug was the only other person who knew about the operation.

Katherine Smith and the other team member then reviewed with Doug what he remembered and what he reported from the CIA "Eyes Only" file he saw while he worked at the CIA. He recalled for them how he was given access to the file and what he remembered. He recognized the CIA source code as indicating the information came from the Israeli Institute for Intelligence and Special Operations (Mossad) but did not include a name for the mole or indicate who the mole was spying for. The CIA claimed they did not have high confidence in the credibility of the information. Doug was given SA Smith's cell phone number and told to contact her if he developed any information.

The Special Team had a list of all the people who worked in or for the White House. They were already checking with the National Security Agency (NSA) to identify any telephone calls with a foreign source placed or received by any of the people on the list. This information would take some time to retrieve. If they came up with anything of interest, they would let Doug know so he could target his efforts inside the White House. Smith then took Doug back to the convenience store where he had left his car. He was a little late getting home. Blair had fixed dinner and was getting Bobby and Charley ready for bed.

The FBI does not have a formal information-sharing relationship with the Mossad. Their contact is usually handled by the CIA. In this case, the Bureau could not put in a request for the Agency to ask for more information, if any, from the Mossad. This would have to be done through backchannels. The FBI has legal attachés in Jerusalem, but their involvement could jeopardize the investigation and even the separate investigation into the leak inside the FBI.

While Doug was in the West Wing doing his re-interviews, he also had the opportunity to observe the contacts between staff members and sometimes visitors. The First Lady's office was in the East Wing, but she was almost always in the West Wing. She appeared to be in constant consultation with the chief of staff and the deputy chief of staff. The deputy chief did not report to the chief of staff. Instead, the deputy apparently reported direct to the president and to his wife, Dr. Jill Biden. It was a strange staffing arrangement. Important visitors met with the president in the Oval Office, and he held meetings in the Cabinet Room; otherwise, he was rarely seen in the West Wing. It caused Doug to wonder if this trio was the Oz behind the curtain running the government.

On one occasion, just after the president had met with a few members of Congress, Doug recognized a member of the Democrat House leadership in the

White House mess with a guest. It was Jenny Ling. She noticed SA Gregory and looked stunned. He ignored her and decided he would leave it up to the FBI agent who now handled her to inquire about her presence in the WH. She was not a known security problem, so there was no reason she could not be cleared to visit the White House. The fact she was an FBI informant did not disqualify her from being there.

About a week after his visit with SA Katherine Smith, Doug received another call from her. She said they needed his help and asked him to come by on his way home. This time he drove to the apartment but did not take a direct route. Since the apartment was a kind of safe house, he drove around the area a couple of times to make sure he was not being followed. When he was sure he had no tail, he went to the apartment. This time, a couple of other special agents were there too.

One of the SAs, from the San Francisco office, said to him, "You look an awful lot like an agent who worked on the Red Dragon squad in San Francisco, but I can't connect the name."

Doug admitted to being the agent. He told the SF agent, "I had a name change after I left there."

The special team decided they needed more information from the Mossad, but even a backchannel contact with someone from the Mossad in the US could tip off the CIA to what the FBI was up to. Instead, they needed someone to go to Israel and get more information, if there was any. Since Doug had seen the

CIA file, they thought he was the best person to ask the Mossad for it. The deputy director approved the trip. On his way home, Doug wondered how he was going to explain a trip to Jerusalem to Blair.

Blair was no longer surprised by anything Doug came home with. She recognized from the beginning of their relationship he had a special talent for getting into unusual situations. She was proud of his work. Her only advice was to be careful overseas. His family needed him at home.

Arraignments were made for Doug to fly from Dulles International Airport to the Ben Gurion Airport near Tel Aviv on a Saturday night. The deputy director of the FBI had personally called the director of Mossad to arrange for a Sunday morning meeting. The agents who are assigned to the WH were told Doug would be on personal leave for a few days.

Doug's arrival in Tel Aviv was delayed almost an hour because of missile strikes from Gaza being fired into Israel. When Doug landed, he was met by a driver from Mossad who got him waived through customs and immigration, and then drove him direct to Mossad headquarters in Tel Aviv. On arrival, he met with the head of services. Doug greeted his host with "Boker tov." He got a greeting in Yiddish in return.

His host then asked Doug how he could help him. The Mossad official had no advance information about the reason for the visit, only that it was a backchannel request for help. Doug proceeded to tell him about how he came to see the CIA file on a mole in the White House and the fallout from the dissemination to the FBI. Doug had been able to identify the Mossad as the source of the intelligence, but the CIA refused to discuss it further with the Bureau because they did not feel it was credible. The head of services said, "Sometimes I think the people at the CIA are idiots. Their problem is they recruit people based on social justice reasons instead of the looking for people with a talent to be in this business."

He then told Doug he would check to see if the information the CIA had did come from the Mossad. If it did, he would be able to confirm whatever was disseminated to the CIA. If it came from his agency, and there is more information, he would have to check with his superiors about releasing the additional information. It would probably take a couple of days before he had an answer for Doug. He suggested Doug stay in a hotel in Tel Aviv and stay alert about the Palestinian missile launches.

Doug checked into the Crown Plaza Tel Aviv Beach, thinking it might be less of a target than the Hilton where Americans usually stay. Of course, he was assuming the Iranian missiles, fired by Palestinians from Gaza, were even capable of targeting certain buildings. It appeared more like they were just randomly firing the missiles into Israel. Fortunately, the Iron Dome defense system employed by the Israeli Army is able to intercept the incoming missiles at about an 86 percent kill rate, at a cost of $40,000 (US) per missile.

The overnight flight had left Doug drained of energy, but he knew better than to go to bed. Since there were no siren warnings, he decided to walk the beach area near the hotel. The fresh air was invigorating. At 5 o'clock, he called Blair. There is a seven-hour time difference between Israel and Virginia, so he knew Blair would have the boys ready for the day. She was glad to know he arrived safely and was staying close by the hotel. Doug spoke to the twins and they recognized their dad's voice on the telephone. After calling home, he decided to eat in the hotel and to turn in early. Part of his first evening in Tel Aviv was spent in a shelter at the hotel because of a Red Alert.

Doug had been warned by the Mossad not to plan a sight-seeing trip to Jerusalem. The Palestinians there were protesting Israel's bombing strikes on the missile sites in Gaza. Between the protests and the missile strikes, it was not a good time for tourists to be visiting historic sites. Since the weather in Tel Aviv was nice, Doug thought he would just walk around the beach near the hotel. There was no chance to do that back in Virginia.

He was up early the next morning. After breakfast, he went for his walk. It was a busy morning on the streets of Tel Aviv but there was no sign there was any incoming missiles. Doug noticed two men working on a light pole near the hotel, but something did not feel right to him. The men did not appear to have the right kind of equipment for whatever it they were trying to do. Then every time a police cruiser or military patrol car came down the street, the men would stop working and disappear for a few minutes. He thought this was very strange. Doug could not read the Hebrew lettering on their truck, so all he could do was make a note of a description of the truck and the men and write down the license plate number. A few minutes later, the men saw Doug watching them, and they decided to leave. Doug did not know what they were doing, but he found it strange enough he decided to report it. He went back to the hotel and called the police. About fifteen minutes after his call, the police came to the hotel to interview him. He showed the police the pole the men had been working on and told them what he had observed. They thanked him and said they would take it from there.

Doug was getting bored watching television and taking walks, but on the third day, the Mossad called and said they were ready to see him again. They sent the same driver for him who picked him up at the airport. This time, there were two people at Mossad to brief Doug. Yes, they had disseminated information to the CIA about the possibly being a mole in the White House. No, they did not identify the mole for the CIA or their source for the information. The CIA did not come back to them to see if there was any additional information the Mossad would share.

Doug asked, "Is there more information you can share about the mole?"

The Mossad agents briefing Doug told him there was some additional information they did not share with the CIA for fear of compromising their source. Mossad will not put the information in writing, but they were willing to verbally share it with Doug, if he would assure them he would only refer to the source as "an Iranian government official." Doug agreed to keep their confidence.

The Mossad agents briefing him proceeded to tell Doug the source is an Iranian foreign ministry official, and the mole is believed to have some connection to a former high-ranking official in the US State Department. The Iranian code name for the mole is "Carline." Because of the code name, the Mossad thinks the mole is female. In Farsi, the name Carline is a noun for "a feisty woman."

The agents said the additional information could be used by the FBI in their attempt to identify the mole, but it was not to be disseminated. Reflecting back on what happened to him when he was working at the CIA, Doug wondered if the CIA was just doing just what the Mossad is now doing: limiting distribution of the intelligence for a legitimate reason. The difference is the Israelis do not have a duty to be forthcoming on criminal activity in the US, while the CIA did. Besides, the agency did not have any source information except which country gave them the information. To Doug, it was like the difference between apples and oranges.

The Mossad agents went on to tell Doug the Israeli police had asked them to thank him for being so observant and reporting the two workman he saw at the light pole. One of the policemen, among the first to arrive, was a bomb expert. He immediately recognized the two were installing a remotely controlled improvised explosive device (IED). They were apparently scared off before they could finish. Because of Doug's description of their truck and its tag number, the police spotted and stopped the truck just a few miles from the city. One of the workmen was from Hamas, and the other was an Iranian. The police were shot at by the Iranian and returned fire. The Iranian was killed, but the Palestinian was in custody. Doug's curiosity and perseverance had stopped what could have become a major terrorist incident.

Doug was asked to be ready early the next day for his departure. He assumed it was because of security reasons. He was ready to return home. When the driver picked him up at the hotel, he was told they were going to make a diversion on the way to the airport. The prime minister was visiting the Israeli Defense Force (IDF)) headquarters in Tel Aviv and wanted to meet Doug. It would only take a few minutes. Needless to say, Doug was surprised.

After only a few minutes in a waiting area at the IDF, Doug was ushered into the Office of the Chief of Staff of the Israeli Army where he was greeted by the Prime Minister (PM), Benjamin Netanyahu. The PM told Doug, when he heard about his involvement in stopping the terrorists from planting the IED in Tel Aviv and learned from the Mossad about the problem Doug had been through with the Israeli intelligence concerning a mole in the WH, he wanted to meet and thank him. The PM agreed to take a picture with Doug. After a brief conversation, Doug was escorted back to the car and sent on his way to Ben Gurion Airport. The visit had been a pleasant surprise to him.

⇥⇥ Chapter 25 ⇤⇤

Blair and the boys picked Dad up at Dulles. They were glad he was home. He was glad to be back too. Because of the time difference, it had been a long day for him, but Blair wanted to hear all about it. Of course, the whole conversation was about the incident near the hotel and his meeting with Netanyahu. When they got to the house, she fixed a glass of wine for her hero and told him to relax before dinner. He passed out in his favorite chair.

The next morning, Doug was still on Israeli time. He called SA Smith at seven o'clock. She told him to come over as soon as he was ready. The team was already at the apartment and anxious to hear what Doug had to report. Within minutes, he was on his way. He told them it was an interesting trip. Without going into business about spotting the terrorist trying to plant the IED or his brief meeting with the Prime Minister, he briefed the FBI team on the Mossad visits. What they knew now, they did not know before, was the original source of the information about a mole was from someone in the Iranian government, the relationship of the mole to someone who had previously been a high-level State Department official, the mole's code name, and that the Israelis believe the mole was female. The new information would help narrow the investigation.

In the meantime, a separate FBI group would be trying to find where the leak was at the Bureau. Doug was not involved in that investigation.

Doug decided not to return to the White House on Friday. Showing up for work on a Friday, after having been gone all week, might look a little strange. Besides he was exhausted from the trip and needed the rest. On Saturday, Aunt Peggy came by to see her nephews and hoped to catch up on what Doug had been doing. She knew he had gone out of town the previous weekend but did not know why or where he went. Doug could not even tell her about meeting the Israeli prime minister. He sluffed his absence off as just an FBI business trip.

The following Monday morning, it was back to the White House to review personnel security files. This time he set the files of male employees aside. Then he started back through the files of the female employees, just in case he had missed something. He had more information now than before.

A couple of weeks after his report to the special investigative team, Doug received a call from SA Katherine Smith. They had homed in on one particular person, and they wanted to discuss her with Doug. He stopped at the apartment on the way home. The name they narrowed the list too is an employee in the WH Communications Office. She is the niece by marriage of an aunt whose father once served as the US Secretary of State. Her father was born in Iran, but he is now an American citizen living here. She is an American Iranian born here but is married and does not use her family name. Doug indicated he recalled interviewing her weeks earlier but did not remember the details. He would take another look at her file to see if there was anything which would help with their investigation. Doug said he would get back to them.

After another review of the suspect's security file, he reported to the team there was nothing unusual in the file or anything which would make him suspect of her. Doug also made it a point to talk to her again, but there was still nothing which caused him any concern. SA Smith told Doug they had received enough information from another source to believe she is Carline and to make her their primary target. Doug suspected the NSA had probably reported telephone calls between her and someone overseas, but he was not part of the team conducting the investigation and did not have a need to know. He had done what he was assigned to do.

The FBI special team would continue their investigation to see if their suspect was an active Iranian spy or had committed any violation of law in her official duties. The Iranians may have recruited her to spy, but if she has not yet disseminated anything to them, there was no way to charge her with anything. In any event, it looked like Doug's days in the White House were numbered. The investigators no longer needed "eyes and ears" inside the WH.

➤➤ Chapter 26 ◄◄

A few days later, there was another call from the seat of government for Doug to come in and talk to the deputy director. This time he knew what it was about. What he did not know was what was next. Doug and Blair had discussed every possible option, but they knew in the end, it would depend largely on the Bureau's needs.

The deputy director told Doug he was impressed with Doug's record as an agent and had received word about his spotting two terrorists trying to place an IED in Tel Aviv and his meeting with the prime minister. Director Wray was informed about these two events, and he too was very pleased. The deputy director then proceeded to tell SA Gregory his assignment to the White House was no longer needed and they would find him another assignment. The two talked at length about what Doug wanted to do in the FBI. Doug mentioned his wife was six months pregnant, and they really did not want to move until after the baby was born. The deputy director then asked Doug if, after their baby is born, he would be willing to take an administrative position in a field office. This was inevitable, unless he wanted to continue to be a brick agent. Doug told the deputy director he and Blair had discussed this and they would be comfortable with an administrative assignment. The only caveat his wife had was she would not take her children to live in New York City. This brought a smile to the face of the deputy director, but he made no comment.

The FBI deputy director then suggested to Doug if he was willing to do some traveling, they could bring him into the SOG, and put him on the inspection staff. Most of the travel would be to field offices in the continental US, and the inspection trips typically last five days to a week. An inspection team makes one or two trips a month. The rest of the time they were in Washington, DC, writing reports. Occasionally the duties involve a trip overseas. The assignment to the inspection staff would be for about six months, after which he would be considered for transfer to a field office as an assistant special agent in charge (ASAC). The assignments as an ASAC typically last one to two years. It would be somewhat of a lifestyle change for the Gregory's, but Doug liked the idea of not moving from their home in Virginia just now.

Doug finished out his temporary assignment at the White House, staying until the end of the week. It looked less suspicious than just disappearing. He had made a number of friends on the WH staff, and one never knows when he might need their help. Blair was content with the decision for Doug to join the inspection staff. COVID-19 restrictions were easing, and she would be able to hire outside help to clean and take care of the house. She might even be able to find a part-time nannie to help with the boys until she has her baby and gets back on her feet. Things seemed to have been happening too fast but maybe now things will get back to being somewhat normal. Returning to normal would start with a family vacation. They had not had one since their honeymoon trip across country between Doug's assignments in San Francisco and Washington, DC.

Doug had never been to Florida, and Blair wanted to show him where she grew up. He took annual leave from the FBI, and they piled into Blair's SUV, heading down I-95 to the Sunshine State. On the way, they decided to spend a day in Savannah, Georgia. They arrived late the first evening of their trip and got settled in the hotel. They next morning, they did some sightseeing on their own. The boys were not yet old enough to take in the usual tourist sites. The azaleas were still in bloom, so they spent some time letting the Bobby and Charley play in Forsyth Park. In the afternoon, they put the boys in their stroller and took them for a walk along the riverfront. The twins seemed fascinated by the big ships plying the Savanah River. After dinner, they all tuned in early.

The following morning, it was back on the interstate. The next stop would be Orlando, Florida. They checked into the Contemporary Hotel at Disney World. The Disney characters walking around the hotel captured the attention of both boys. In the morning, they went to the Magic Kingdom. There were only a few rides they could take the twins on, but again the characters were what was of interest to the two-year-old's. Doug and Blair were enjoying the boys enjoy themselves. After a nap back in the hotel, it was time to introduce the boys to the hotel swimming pool. It sure was different in Florida than in Virginia. The State was "open," and you did not have to wear a COVID-19 mask. Needless to say, the children were both exhausted and slept through the evening fireworks.

Now on the I-4 corridor, which divides the state geographically, they headed toward Tampa and then took I-75 South to Sarasota. They had booked accommodations on Siesta Key near the public beach. It was too warm to go to the beach in the afternoon. Siesta Key is regularly touted to be one of the best beaches in the United States, but despite being crowded this time of year, social distancing was still being observed by most people.

After an overnight rest, they were ready to take their pent-up energy to the beach. Blair had spent a lot of time on the beach at Siesta Key during her high school years. For Doug, being on the beach reminded him of the beach in Tel Aviv, only this beach was nicer. Bobby and Charley were in their element. They were all in love with the beach. Before noon, they had enough sun and went back to their apartment for naps. In the afternoon, Blair took them on drive around Sarasota to show them where she grew up. Sarasota had changed a lot, but it still was one of the nicest cities in Florida.

Morning trips to the beach became a daily routine. In the afternoon, they put the boys in their stroller and took them to Mote Marine, Sarasota Jungle Gardens, and the Big Cat Gulf Coast Sanctuary. Blair took Doug by the Pine View School, where she went to middle and high school. In telling Doug about her high school experiences, she mentioned she was particularly fond of one of the administrators, Dr. Brenda George. After a week of enjoying themselves, it was time to head back home. The trip back to Virginia was not as much fun as the trip to Florida, but they were glad to get home. They had taken a lot of pictures, so now Blair and Aunt Peggy would have to make albums for each of the boys.

It took the weekend for Doug to recover from the vacation trip, but the following Monday he reported to the inspection division. He was in a new realm. This division reports through an associate deputy director (ADD), a Bureau official who Doug had not before been directly involved. There were three squads of agents and support people assigned to the division. Doug was assigned the Squad Number Two. While most of the time a squad worked as a standalone team, it could be supplemented by someone from one of the other squads if they were inspecting a large field office or an office with a major problem. Doug could expect to be used on occasion by one of the other squads. Occasionally, a member one of the inspection squads might be tasked for a solo assignment.

⤜⤜ Chapter 27 ⤛⤛

D oug's first trip as a member of his inspection squad was to the field office in Cincinnati, Ohio. He would be assigned to review both some office administration procedures and the supervision of case files. He could expect to be gone about five nights. On Sunday night, the squad assembled in a hotel near the Cincinnati office and received their final instructions. Unannounced, the following morning they descended on the field office. Doug and another team member were tasked to drive to Columbus, Ohio, for an inspection of the resident agency. This was Doug's first visit back to Columbus since he graduated from Ohio State and entered the FBI. Senior resident agent Danny Johnson had long since retired. A couple of the agents still working there remembered Doug from when he applied for the FBI through the Columbus RA.

Doug had an RA inspection checklist, which he used to conduct his inspection. It only took a few hours for the two agents to complete their work, but since they got a late start, it was already late in the day when they finished—too late to drive back to Cincinnati. After the inspection of the RA, Doug took the other agent on a tour of his Alma Mater. Much of The Ohio

State University campus had changed, but the Oval and University Hall were still the most beautiful part of it. In the evening, they had dinner in Germantown at a restaurant, which was Doug's favorite after law school. Early the next morning, they headed south on I-75 for "The Queen City." There were still a couple of days' work in the field office. Doug worked late into Thursday evening and was sent back to DC the next morning. It had been a busy week.

Blair had things under control at home. She had arranged for a clearing service to come in once a week and found an English nannie to come in on weekdays to help care for the twins. The boys were growing up fast. Blair was even a little surprised how much easier it was for her having help around the house. When Doug got home from Cincinnati, he failed to even notice how tidy everything was.

The conversation over dinner was all about the trip and going back to Ohio State. After a glass of wine and an excellent dinner, Doug was prepared for an early turn in. Blair watched a little more of the evening news, but once the boys were in bed she was ready to call it a night too.

On Saturday morning, Aunt Peggy came by to check on the Gregory's. Besides seeing Bobby and Charley, she was anxious to find out what was going on with Doug. She missed seeing him in the WH mess. Margaret was a very perceptive person and knew something was going on with his career. Doug told her the additional help he was giving the agents assigned at the WH was no longer required. His new job gave him an opportunity for advancement.

Doug suggested, if Margaret was interested in meeting some of his friends, he had a middle-aged widower on his squad whom she might enjoy seeing. His wife died a few months ago, so he was not looking to get married. He seems like a pretty solid individual and someone who would be a lot of fun. Margaret told Doug and Blair she has been seeing a Democrat Congressman from New Jersey. It's not a serious relationship, but it has taken up some of her evenings. On weekends, he goes back to his district, so the best time to introduce her to one of Doug's fellow special agents would be on a Saturday night. Blair then suggested Doug invite the agent for dinner on a weekend. Doug said he would work on it.

It was Memorial Day weekend, and Doug was just back from his first inspection trip, so nothing was planned for Monday. Doug would be at home with Blair and the boys. It also gave him the chance to meet the boys' new nannie. Her name is Barbara, and she was the widow of a young US Navy officer killed in the bombing of the USS Cole in Aden, Yemen, back in 2000. Prior to marrying the American sailor, she was a nannie for some of the members of the Royal family in England. Since her husband's death, she worked for several prominent families in the Washington, DC, area. Blair dubbed her as Lady Barbara.

Back in the office after the trip to the Cincinnati field office, Doug was told the following week he would be attached to Inspection Squad One for an inspection of the Los Angeles Division. This was a much larger division than Cincinnati, so they needed to supplement the inspection team. As low man on the totem pole in the inspection division, he knew he would be tasked. On Sunday, Doug and the inspection team members flew to the West Coast.

As had been done on his previous inspection trip, he and another team member were dispatched to inspect the RA in Orange County. Driving in California was not quite as easy as it was in Ohio. Just getting to RA took a good part of the morning. They finished their inspection the following afternoon and then headed back to the field office. The next two days Doug was in the LA field office reviewing FD 302s prepared by agents working interview leads on applicants for FBI employment and security clearances. He was surprised to see the recent report of an interview done of a person who knew "Carline." She was originally from southern California. Doug checked the file to see who generated the lead and was glad to see it came from the deputy director and not regular channels. This meant the case on a mole in the WH still has limited access in the Bureau. On Friday, Doug was released to return to Washington, DC.

On Monday, after the trip to LA, Doug learned his Squad Two was scheduled to inspect the San Antonio field office the following week. Doug was learning why assignments to the inspection division usually were only for six months. During the first few weeks of his transfer to this assignment, he was gone from home more days than he would be working in Washington, DC. The following Sunday, it was off to San Antonio, Texas.

Chapter 28

Still the newest agent assigned to his squad, again Doug drew the inspection of an RA. This time it was the office in Austin where they have ASAC in charge of the office. He called Blair and asked her to make contact with Bobby and Charley's blood relatives to see if he could meet with any of them for dinner. Doug was a proud father who kept plenty of pictures of the boys on his personal cell phone. He thought they might enjoy seeing pictures of the twins.

This time he did not have a partner to accompany him. He was on his own, but he had his RA inspection checklist and two RA inspections under his belt. He drove from San Antonio to Austin on Monday and went to work. Blair called him to say she had talked to the sister of Shirley's husband and arranged for Doug to meet the aunt and her husband for dinner.

Doug showed them his picture collection. The boys' birth aunt and uncle showed little interest in how the boys were doing. She commented the boys looked more like Doug than Shirley's husband. The aunt went on to comment her brother told her he thought Shirley was already pregnant when he married her. The straw that broke the camel's back was when Shirley insisted on naming the twins, Robert and Charles. The husband believed someone by the name of Robert Charles Allen was the real father. The aunt and uncle were glad Shirley's friend, Blair Reed, agreed to adopt them. There was no need for Doug to fill them in on the history. It was a short evening.

Doug still had some work to do in the RA on Tuesday, so he did not leave Austin until the afternoon. From there he drove to the RA in Del Rio, Texas. It was about a three and one-half hours' drive. Doug was enamored by the Lady Bird flowers he saw along the highway. There were huge expanses sprinkled with blooms of indigo, periwinkle, scarlet, coral, and gold. It was a beautiful sight.

He arrived in Del Rio and made a quick stop to introduce himself to the senior resident agent. By now, the whole San Antonio division knew they were under inspection. The SRA suggested they have dinner with the Val Verde County Sheriff. The RA had some unique problems due to the immigration problems taking place along the border with Mexico, and the sheriff was their biggest ally.

While the Del Rio RA covered a seven-county area of south Texas, only two of the counties are on the border with Mexico, but the other counties are close enough to be impacted by the same issues. Del Rio is the major city in Val Verde County, which is opposite Acuna Ciudad. Eagle Pass, Texas, in Maverick County, is opposite Piedras Negras in Mexico. Both Mexican cities are in the Coahuila State, which is the third most populated state in Mexico. The state is controlled by the Las Zeta Cartel. The issues with the Zetas were the problem the SRA wanted to discuss with Doug.

All ports of entry were closed to immigrants trying to enter the United States. This allowed the Biden administration to claim the border with Mexico was closed. However, nothing could be further than the truth. Val Verde County's border with the Coahuila State is 110 miles long. There are only four miles of the Trump border fence in Val Verde County. Elsewhere, the fencing is mostly just barrier fence to prevent vehicles driving into the US. The Rio Grande River runs almost the entire length of the border of Val Verde County and Mexico, but there are points where the river is so shallow people can drive or walk across it.

The sheriff added the US Border Patrol is no longer able to prevent illegals from crossing into Val Verde or Maverick County because they are tied up processing and babysitting the illegals who cross into the US between the ports of entry. He has only four deputies on duty at any one time along the Val Verde County border with Mexico, and they spend almost all their time rescuing immigrants crossing the river. Recently, on one day alone, they rescued 600 people crossing the border illegally, but there is no telling how many illegals entered the US at other places along the Val Verde County border and were not processed by the sheriff. Maverick County, Texas, has the same problem.

Since Las Zeta controls the border in Coahuila State, they maintain lookouts to spot US law enforcement. The authorities on the Texas side of the border can also see and watch the cartel spotters. The cartel is mainly involved in two operations; one is the human trafficking of illegals. The "Cayotes" bring the illegals to the Mexican side of the river where it is shallow and dump them. The immigrants then have to swim or walk across the border. This ties up the sheriff's resources to rescue these people while other cartel operators find other border places not protected by law enforcement to brings drugs into the US. It is a large-scale operation for the cartels, which is made easy because of American immigration policies. The amount of money the cartels make from human trafficking and drugs amounts to millions of dollars a day. It is this money, which breeds the corruption in Mexico. Many Mexican officials are on the take "to just look the other way." The cartels can then operate with impunity in Mexico.

The cartels have also expanded their operations on the US side of the border. The sheriff said there were thirteen Las Zeta gangs in Las Verdes County that help the Mexican cartels by acting as enforcers for the cartels on the American side of the border. They are also involved in funneling bribe money to US officials. Information had been received from an informant that huge amounts of cartel money was being funneled to Democrat political candidates as the result of a tacit agreement struck with the Biden administration. This agreement was made even before the administration announced the current policies, which allow almost unrestricted illegal immigration across the Mexican border.

Doug was not sure what he could do with the information he got from the sheriff and the SRA, except to document it in his inspection report of the RA. The FBI does not set or control immigration policy. This is the prerogative of the Department of Homeland Security. The next morning, Doug was in the RA going through his RA inspection checklist. Before Doug left to drive back to San Antonio, the SRA took Doug to a crossing point to watch the illegal immigrants crossing the river. There were two deputies pulling people from the river. The two FBI agents had to help rescue the immigrants as they arrived on the US side of the border. Doug took pictures with his cell phone. Late in the afternoon, he drove back to the field office in San Antonio. Doug spent the next day with the inspection team in San Antonio and then flew back to DC mid-day on Friday. It had been another busy week for him.

It was great to be home for the weekend. Blair and the boys were glad to see him, and it was good to see Aunt Peggy too. Blair planned a special Saturday night dinner for them. After eating mostly fast food for a week, Doug was appreciative his wife was a chef extraordinaire. Even Margaret was impressed with Blair's cooking skills and brought flowers for the occasion. Nothing was said at dinner about his meeting in Austin, but they did talk about what Doug saw at the river. The government may have technically closed the border at the ports of entry, but to say "the border is closed" is an outright lie. The border is like a sieve, and the public is intentionally being misled by the government and the media.

Inspection Squad Two had the week in DC to prepare their report on the San Antonio field office and it's resident agencies. In his part of the report, Doug went into great detail about how the immigration problems along the Texas border was affecting the work of the resident agents in the Del Rio RA. That was all he could do.

Following a week in DC, the next field office his squad was assigned to inspect was the Baltimore division. Doug liked that. He figured since the drive to Baltimore, on the Washington-Baltimore Parkway, was only a little over forty miles and would only take him about an hour and half each way, he could spend some nights at home. However, the night before the inspection, the squad gathered in a Baltimore hotel and Doug drew the Wilmington, Delaware RA to inspect. He would not be home on Monday evening for sure. The drive to Wilmington is seventy-five miles in the wrong direction. Doug arrived at the RA before noon and went to work.

One of the agents in the RA he interviewed about his work was the agent who picked up Hunter Biden's laptop from the computer repairman it had been left with. Doug confirmed the agent had not looked at the material on the laptop since the Bureau needed to first obtain a search warrant before looking at it, but the RA had interviewed the repairman several times since taking possession of the laptop. The repairman had looked what was on the computer and had even copied it. According to the repairman, there was apparently a lot of incriminating information on the computer, but the thing which worried him the most was an email regarding the murder of Seth Rich, in Washington, DC, back in 2016. Having knowledge of the information in the email made the repairman fear for his life.

The rest of the inspection in the Wilmington RA was routine. When he left the next morning, he drove to Dover, Delaware, for the inspection of that RA. He was going in the right direction but was getting even further from the Baltimore office. When he finished in Dover, he headed back to the Baltimore field office. Since the road back was through Washington, DC, he spent the night at home instead of staying in a hotel. Blair and the boys were glad to see Dad, but early the next morning, he was back on the Washington-Baltimore Parkway. The rest of the week was spent in the field office. Late Friday afternoon, the inspection team was sent home.

Doug had only been on the inspection squad a couple of months, and Blair's due date was fast approaching, but the Bureau was experiencing a lot of retirements. Members of the inspection division were being selected for ASAC jobs earlier than anticipated. Doug was told he had been selected to become an ASAC, but for which field office had not yet been determined. He was told to prepare for reassignment in the next sixty days. A week later, Doug was called back to meet with the HR people. This time they told him a position as a legal attaché in Singapore was also opening. Because of his assignment background and Mandarin fluency, he was also being considered for that position. Did he have a preference?

Doug and Blair discussed the options at length. Her due date was probably the first week of August. The reporting date for either position would probably be the first of September. Whatever they decided about his next assignment, he would take leave the month of August. In September, he would begin what would be a new career in the FBI.

Epilogue

The lesson learned by Douglas Gregory during his six years as an FBI special agent was the information given the public by governments, the mainstream media, or allowed by Big Tech on their internet platforms is likely misinformation, wrong, or an outright lie. It is often done intentionally to maintain *control* of the consequences of events. Whether it be the US or a foreign country, a political party, or a major corporation, controlling the consequences is necessary in order to maintain control of the population and the economy. Successful control results in the ultimate goal: *power.*

What SA Gregory discovered was, frequently if you look at the facts and question what might be, instead of just listening to the rhetoric, you may see through what is being fed to you. The COVID-19 pandemic is one of the best examples to prove this point. At the outset of the pandemic, Americans were told by the US government and media, the virus originated in the wet market of Wuhan, China. In fact, the US Government knew gain-of-function research on coronavirus was transferred from the USAMRIID at Fort Detrick, Maryland, to the Wuhan Laboratory of

Virology in China, along with 3.6 million dollars to fund the continuation gain-of-function research. It took two years from the inception of the pandemic for this information to be made public.

Even after the disclosure that the SARS-CV-2 virus was being researched in the laboratory in Wuhan, the media continued to report the virus was likely caused by bats being studied in Wuhan laboratory. When it was reported the virus was man-made, the scenario shifted to an accidental release from the laboratory. Even then "speculation" about COVID-19 being caused by a lab accident was not permitted on Big Tech's platforms. Missing totally from the discussion was the possibility the virus was intentionally released in order to create the world-wide pandemic. Most people acknowledge that China is America's most dangerous adversary. Why was no one willing to consider the virus may have been intentionally released from the Chinese military–controlled laboratory? Why did China immediately impose severe domestic travel restriction but did not stop international travel out of the country? No one seemed to notice China is the least affected country in the world from the pandemic.

At the same time there was a lot of "news" about the trade negotiations between the Trump administration and China, but little attention was paid by the media to the fact the Chinese were not agreeing to anything permanent which would improve the balance of payments for the US. The "Chinese Dream" of becoming the number one economy in the world, at the expense of the Unites States, continued. While in negotiations with Trump's trade advisors the Chinese were deeply engaged in planning to help Joe Biden become the next president. This intentional interference would have significant *intended consequences* both in the presidential election and the post-election economy of the US. To the media and Big Tech, there was nothing here to see. The American public was instead told to be concerned about wearing masks and social distancing.

Following the election of Joe Biden, largely because of voter reaction to the large number of apparent irregularities in the president election, there were a lot of voter fraud allegations. The Chinese were accused of interference, but so were others. In the end, it did not make any difference. The election had its intended consequences, and the Democrats were in *control*. The media told the country Republicans were just unhappy because they lost the election, and what they needed to do was just move on. To maintain control the government and the media then shifted the scenario to a lockdown of Washington, DC, claiming it was necessary in order to avoid right-wing terrorism.

There were few reported threats of protest on the internet, prior to the Electoral College deliberation in the Capitol on January 6, 2021, but the director of the FBI went public about possible right-wing protests at the Capitol. When protestors did enter the Capitol, the media immediately identified them as "Marchers from the Trump rally on the Mall." This was clearly untrue, since the protestors entered the Capitol before the people at the rally even began their march to the Capitol. A half-dozen of the protestors arrested were members of a loosely organized internet group, which has no real membership base. No other right-wing protest groups were ever identified. By managing the disinformation, those in power were able to achieve the *intended consequences—control.*

Then there is the dissemination of information about what is happening on the US–Mexico border. The government and the media are telling Americans the border is closed and everything is under control, while the truth appears to be something else. Big Tech is complicit by censorship of information on its internet platforms to keep the public under control.

Time is the purveyor of the truth, but if you want to know about the truth of an important event when it happens, instead of waiting for someone to discover it, ask yourself questions, research what you can about the facts, and consider the possibilities. Why is the information about on Hunter Biden's laptop about the murder of Seth Rich so devastating the computer repairman is in fear of his life? Why does the Biden administration allow uncontrolled immigration across the Mexican border when they know the cartels are making millions of dollars from human trafficking of immigrants and increased drug trafficking? Consider the possible options. Then discount what you are being told by the government, the media, and Big Tech. Remember, they have a vested interest. If you do this, more often than not, you will understand the truth of what is really happening. Look for the *intended consequences*.